John Hawkins Simpson

Napoleon III On England

John Hawkins Simpson

Napoleon III On England

ISBN/EAN: 9783742863386

Manufactured in Europe, USA, Canada, Australia, Japa

Cover: Foto ©ninafisch / pixelio.de

Manufactured and distributed by brebook publishing software (www.brebook.com)

John Hawkins Simpson

Napoleon III On England

NAPOLEON III.

on

ENGLAND.

SELECTIONS FROM HIS OWN WRITINGS.

Edited and Translated

by

JOHN HAWKINS SIMPSON.

"Coming erlentJ cajl their Jbadows before."

London:
Saunders, Otley, and Co., Conduit Street.
18 6 o.

EDITOR'S PREFACE.

Can we from the writings of Napoleon III., whilst a prince in exile, form any decided opinion as to his real sentiments and intentions with respect to England! To put it in the power of every Englishman calmly to consider this question and answer it for himself-such is the aim of this little volume.

I have carefully selected those passages in the writings of the Imperial author which have direct or indirect reference to this country : the selection has not been made so as to favour any preconceived opinion of my own- l' have scrupulously avoided doing so.

Is it not of vital importance that the man who guides the destinies of France, and of Europe, too, in no small degree, shall be impartially judged by our justice-loving land! It would be hard to estimate the amount of strength and consistency that the cause of Liberty all over the world would derive from a calm and *national* consideration on our part of the entire scope of the relations between England and France. But this cannot be effected unless Englishmen, setting aside prejudices and suspicions, will endeavour to guide themselves by knowledge and reason, instead of being helpless, or worse than helpless, through ignorance and passion.

The inhabitants of this free country are too apt to regard the Emperor's rule in France from an entirely English point of view; that is sure to mislead them, and, being so far mislead, they proceed in the course of error when they come to consider (or rather *not consider)* the nature of his feelings and probable intentions towards their own country. In the writings of Louis Napoleon, published at considerable intervals and under very varied circumstances, all of which have the strongest marks of sincerity, we fail to discover any symptoms of hostility towards England : quite the reverse. Frequently, and without variation, he expresses his admiration of her constitutional government, her power of public opinion; her freedom of th~ press, and his great respect for her Protestant religion; whilst he, from the very first, states that, though theoretically an admirer of a republic, he believes that a monarchical rule is best calculated to further the interests of France.

He writes, "not the ashes only, but also the ideas of the Emperor are to be brought back;" but, that nothing unfriendly or aggressive as regards this country is meant, we gather from this passage relating to Waterloo :-" Waterloo !...... Here the voice of every Frenchman fails, he can only shed tears ! tears to weep with the conquered, tears to weep with the conquerors, who will sooner or later regret having overthrown the only man who made himself a mediator between two hostile ages!"

In all his writings he insists upon it that the Genera.l Treaty of Vienna, June 9, 1815, signed by Austria, Spain, France, England, Portugal, Prussia, Russia, and Sweden, was a futile attempt to procure a balance of power, hy means of arrangements to suit reigning dynasties, and that it was not attempted to frame it to meet the requirements and wishes of nationalities. Every day the people, if not the rulers, of England are coining nearer to ihe same conclusion: so *non-inter,oentionin conti-Mldal disputes* is the growing wish of the English people.

But how can non-intervention be invariably

maintained so long as the Treaty of Vienna, though often broken, remains like a boiling spring whence tho floods of war may any day burst forth / Would not the people of England act wisely if they proceeded calmly to examine this Treaty for themselves (not leaving the initiative with ambassadors or ministers), with a view to settling, once for all, how far they will, and how far they will not, consider themselves bound to preserve its mutilated remains.

That point once decided and frankly avowed, Hungarians, Italians, and all oppressed nationalities will know what to expect and what not to expect from us : our " foreign relations," being settled on a NATIONAL BASIS, will cease to be, as they now are, contradictory and irritating, and we shall not afterwards be disgraced by those " invasion panics " which are loud proclamations of our deficiency iu dignity and moral courage.

J. H. S.

London, Feb. 8th, 1860,

CONTENTS.

	PAGE
Editor's Preface	iii
Napoleonian Ideas	
The Napoleonian Idea	31
Answer to M. de Lamartine	40
Political Reveries	44
The Conservative Party	47
Personal Freedom in England	60
The Slave Trade and the Right of Search	64
Opinion of the Emperor on the Relations between France and the Powers of Europe	61
Historical Fragments-1688 and 1880	67
Our Colonies in the Pacific Ocean	177
Union gives Strength	179
Improvements to be Introduced into our Parliamentary Manners and Habits	191

CONTENTS.

PAGE

Peace , 192

The Boundaries of France as defined by the Treaty of Paris, May 30, 1814, and confirmed by the Vienna Congress, June 9, 1816   197

NAPOLEONIAN IDEAS.

[When Louis Napoleon was thirty-two yean old, be, at the desire of Louis-Phillippe, was expelled from Switzerland: taking refuge in England, be wrote *De, Idle, Napoleoniennes,* dated from London, in July, 1839.)

PREFACE.

The Emperor is no more! but his spirit is not dead. Not having the power to defend his tutelary power by arms, I can at least try to defend his memory by my writings. To enlighten the opinions of men by seeking out the thought which presided over his lofty conceptions, to recall his vast projects, is a task which rejoices my heart, and which consoles me in exile.

* * *

CHAPTER I.

GOVERNME~TS IN GENERAL.

All nations have something in common: they wish to be perfected; each nation has something peculiar to itself: uncomfortable circumstances which paralyse its efforts to attain perfection. * * *
In history we everywhere find these two great phenomena: on the one side, an ever-during system, in accordance with regular progression, which advances and never retraces its steps: this is progress; and on the other hand, on the contrary, we Ree only flexibility and mobility: these are forms of government. * * * Since the creation of the world, there has always been progress. To see the truth of this, we have only to follow up the course which civilization has followed; great men have been its stations; each brings us a degree nearer to the end; and one proceeds from Alexander to

Cresar, from Cmsar to Constantine, from Constantine to Charlemagne, from Charlemagne to Napoleon.

Forms of government, on the contrary, do not follow constant laws. Republics are as old as the world; the right of election and hereditary right have, during ages, disputed for power, and power has rested in turns with those who had on their side science and enlightenment, right or force. * * * The beat government is that which accomplishes its mission well, that is to sa.y, the one which adapts itself to the want of the period, and which, ta.king its form from the present state of society, employs the means necessary to open a. level and easy road for civilization which advances.

I say it with regret, at this day I see only two governments which will accomplish the mission entrusted to them by Providence : the two colossi of the world, the one at the extremity of the new, the other at the extremity of the old. Whilst our old European centre is like a. volcano consuming itself within its own crater, the eastern and the western nations are marching, without halting, towards perfection, the one by the will of a single individual, the other by liberty.

Providence has confided to the United States of America the task of peopling and civilizing all that immense territory which stretches from the Atlantic to the South Sea, and from the North Pole to the equator. The government, which is only one of simple administration, has, hitherto, had nothing to do but put in practice this old adage, *laisserfaire, laisserpasser,* to favour the irresistible instinct which urges towards the west the peoples of America.

In Russia, to the imperial dynasty are to be attributed all those progressions which, within a century and a half, have wrested this vast empire from barbarism. The imperial power has to contend with the old prejudices of our old Europe; it must centralize, as much as possible, in the hands of one man, the forces of the State, in order to destroy all the abuses which are perpetuated under the shelter of communal and feudal exemptions. Only from such a power can the East receive the ameliorations which it is waiting for.

But thou, France of Henri IV., of Louis XIV., of Carnot, of Napoleon, thou who wast ever for the west of Europe the source whence came progress, thou who possessest the two supports of empires, the genius of the arts of peace, and the genius of war, hast thou no longer a mission to fulfil ! Wilt thou always exhaust thy force and thy energy in ceaseless conflict with thine own children! No, such cannot be thy destiny ; soon shall come the day when, in order to govern thee, it must be understood that thy *role* is to cast into all treaties thy sword of Brennus in favour of cixilization.

CHAPTER II.

GENERAL IDEAS.

When ideas, which have governed the world during lengthened periods, lose, by the necessary transformation of societies, their force and their empire, new ones arise, destined to take the place of those which preceded them. Although they contain within themselves the germ of reorganization, they nevertheless first proceed to disorganization.

● ● ● ●

Napoleon, when he arrived on the scene of the world, saw that it was his *rôle* to be the revolution"s testamentary executor. The destroying fire of parties had gone out, and when the revolution dying, but not subdued, bequeathed to Napoleon the accomplishment of its last wishes, it surely said to him : " Establish on solid bases the chief results of my efforts, unite once more Frenchmen now divided, repulse feudal Europe leagued against me, heal my wounds, enlighten the nations, carry out in breadth that which I would have done in depth; be for Europe what I have been for France; and even if you have to shed your blood round the tree of civilization, to see your projects misconstrued, and your relatives countryless wanderers over the world, never abandon the sacred cause of the French people, and cause it to triumph by all the means which genius gives birth to, which humanity approves."

This grand mission Napoleon accomplished to the utmost. His task was a difficult one. It was necessary to establish society, still boiling with hatred and rancour, on new principles: to use, for the purpose of consolidating, the same instruments which up to that time had been grasped only for destruction.

The common lot of every new truth which rises is to terrify, and not to attract, to wound instead of convincing. It bounds forward with greater strength the longer it has been repressed; having obstacles to overcome, it must strive to overturn, until, understood and adopted by the majority, it becomes the base of a new social order.

• • • •

The Emperor Napoleon has helped more than any other to hasten the reign of liberty, by preserving the moral influence of the revolution, and diminishing the fears which it inspired.[1]

Without the Consulate and the Empire, the revolution would have been only a grand drama leaving grand recollections, but few traces. • • •
He purified the reeolution, eatabliskfd Icings, and ennobled nations, to use his own words. He purified the revolution, by separating the truths, which he made to triumph, from the passions which, in the general delirium, had obscured them ; he established kings, by making power honoured and respectable ; he ennobled the nations, by making them know their power, and giving them those institutions which elevate men in their own eyes. The Emperor must be considered the Messiah of new ideas. For, it must be said, in the moments which immediately follow a social

---

[1] The fears which the French Revolution inspired in those sovereigns, who in their dominions put a stop to the improvements which ha.d been introduced before 1789, by Joseph II. in Austria, and by Leopold in Italy.

earthquake, what is essential is, not to put in practice principles of subtle theory, but to grasp the genius of regeneration, to identify oneself with the sentiments of the people, and to direct it boldly towards the end which it wishes to reach.

  * * * *

"I don't wish," said Napoleon, "to fall into the error of men who are all for the modem systems, to believe that I, by myself alone and by my ideas, constitute the wisdom of nations. The genius of a workman consists in knowing how to make use of the materials which he has at hand."

He re-established religion, but without making the clergy a means of governing.

  * * * *

He said to the nation, " Do you desire an hereditary power?" and the nation answered in the affirmative by four million votes.

  * * * *

To supply stability and gradual progression, the want of which is the greatest defect of democratic republics, he had to create an hereditary family which should be the protector of the interests of all, but its power was to be based only on the nation's democratic spirit.

"Have I then reigned over dwarfs in intellect, that they have so little understood me!" exclaimed Napoleon at St. Helena, in a fretful moment•••... Let his spirit be consoled! The masses have long since rendered him justice; each passing day, as it discovers one of the miseries which he healed, an evil which he extirpated, sufficiently explains his noble projects. And his grand thoughts, which shine all the brighter through the surrounding darkness, are as beacons of light, pointing out to us, in the midst of clouds and tempests, security in the future!

CHAPTER III.

HOME AFFAIRS.

IT has nearly always happened that, in times of trouble, oppressed people have claimed liberty as their right, and, once they have obtained it, have refused it to those who were their oppressors. In England, in the XVIIth century, there was a religious and republican sect, which, persecuted by the intolerance of the clergy and of the government, decided upon abandoning the land of its ancestors to go beyond the sea, into a world without inhabitants, to enjoy that sweet and holy liberty which the old world denied to it. Victims of intolerance, well knowing the ills which it inflicts, ah! surely, in the country which they are about to found, these independent men will be more just than their oppressors. But, inconsistency of the human heart! the first law of the

Puritans, forming a new society in the State of Massachusetts, is-penalty of death to those who depart from their religious doctrine!

Let us admire the spirit of Napoleon, he was never exclusive nor intolerant. Above small party-passions, generous as the people he was called upon to govern, the Emperor always expressed this maxim: that in politics it is nec~ssary to redress grievances, never to avenge them.

•　　•　　•　　•

The first qualification necessary in a people which aspires to a free form of government, is respect for law.

•　　•　　*　　•

His government did not fall into the error, common to so many others, of separating the interests of the soul from those of the body, by casting back the first into the region of chimeras, and admitting only the second into real existence. Napoleon, on the contrary, by giving an impulse to all elevated passions, by showing that merit and virtue led to riches and to honours, proved to the people that the noble sentiments of the heart of man are really the standards of material interests well understood; just as the Christian moral law is sublime, because, even like a civil law;.it is the surest guide which we can follow, the best counsellor for our private interests.

● ● ●

Under the Empire, centralization was the only way in which France could be settled, a stable *rBgime* established and the whole country rendered compact, able at once to resist Europe, and, later, to keep steady under a reign of liberty. Extreme centralization, under the Empire, should therefore not be looked upon as a definitive and fixed system, but rather as a means by which to attain an end.

*   *   *   *

At the commencement of the Consulate, Pitt, our terrible adversary, saw in the want of money and of credit the impending ruin of France. He knew not how great were the resources which it possessed, and which an able ruler could command. A single year, in fact, sufficed for Napoleon, after the 18 *brumaire,* to regulate the collection of revenue, in such a way that doing away~with violent measures, he met all expences, diminished imposts, restored value to the coin of the realm, and possessed in his portfolio means to the amount of 300 millions.

"Finance based upon a good system of agriculture is inexhaustible," said the first Consul.¹ Facts have shown that he was right.

* * * *

France should congratulate herself that the system of loans, which now crushes England, was never to any extent resorted to under the Empire. Napoleon established principles quite the reverse, for by a special law he fixed 80 millions as the maximum for the public debt.

* * * *

The Emperor estimated that France required a, budget of 800 millions in time of war, and 600 millions in time of peace. Under the Empire, the budget never exceeded the above-stated sums, except after the reverse at Moscow.

* * * *

The amelioration of the condition of the poor classes was one of the chief objects of the Emperor.

* * * *

He orderld the prefets to report to him who those proprietors were who distinguished themselves as agriculturists, whether by a system of

¹ Letter of Napoleon to the King of England.

tillage better understood and more in accordance with reason, or by a more careful attention to the breeding and improvement of farm stock. In the departments where agriculture was backward, the good proprietors were urged to send their sons to study the method pursued in those departments where agriculture flourished. Praises and distinctions were awarded to those who had profited most by so doing.

* * *

The conscription, which unfortunately weighed so heavily on France because of the prolongation of the war, was one of the greatest institutions of the age. Not only did it consecrate the principle of equality, but as General Foy said, "it must be the palladium of our independence, because, infusing the nation into the army and the army into the nation, it furnishes the country with inexhaustible resources for defence."

* * *

The Emperor said, " A nation, when repelling an invasion, is never in want of men, but it often lacks soldiers."

* * * *

England has for a long time shone as a beautiful

spectacle of parliamentary liberty. But what is the element of the English constitution, what is the base of the edifice? the aristocracy. Suppress it, and in England there will be nothing organized.

● ● ● ●

" I wish to erect in France a civil order. Hitherto there have been in the world but two powers, military and ecclesiastic. The barbarians who invaded the Roman Empire could form no solid establishment, because they had no body of priests, no civil *order."-Speeck* of *the Emperor to the Council* of *State.*

CHAPTER IV.

FOREIGN AFFAIRS.

There are three ways in which we may regard the relations of France with foreign governments. They ma.y be thus arranged :-

There is a blind and passionate policy, which would throw down the gauntlet to Europe, and dethrone all kings.

There is another, the exact opposite to this, and which consists in maintaining peace, in purchasing the friendship of sovereigns at the expense of the honour and interests of the country.

Lastly, there is a third policy, which frankly offers the alliance of France to all governments which will progress with it towaras the attainment of interests common to all.

Adopt the first, and you will have no truce, no peace; adopt the second, there will be no war, but there will be no independence; adopt the third, there will be no dishonourable peace, no universal war.

The third system is the Napoleonian policy; it is that which the Emperor put into practice during the whole of his career. If Napoleon fell notwithstanding, his fall was the result of causes which we will explain further on ; but certain it is, without he had adopted this policy, he never would have triumphed over the attacks of Europe.

*   *   *   *

Ever since 1796, when, with 30,000 men, he conquered Italy, he was not only a great general, but a profound politician. The Directory, in its ignorance of matters, sends an order to General Bonaparte to dethrone the King of Sardinia, and to march upon Rome, leaving in his rear 80,000 Austrians who were debouching from the Tyrol. Napoleon frees himself from instructions so badly calculated. He concludes an alliance offensive and defensive with the King of Piedmont, makes a treaty with the Pope, and fights the Austrians : the fruit of this conduct is the peace of Oampo-Formio. At last, a few years only have rolled by, and Napoleon, lately the head of a State at war with the whole of

Europe, unites under the tricolour flag, to march upon Moscow, Prussians, Hanoverians, Hollanders, Saxons, Westphalians, Poles, Austrians, the people of Wurtemburg, Bavarians, Swiss, Lombards, Tuscans, Neap?litans, &c., &c.

It is by the agglomeration of all these peoples united under his orders, that one can judge of the political ability of the Emperor. If he did not succeed at Moscow, it is not because his combinations were badly effected: fate and the elements were required to league together against him.

* * * *

To assure the independence of France, to establish a European peace on a solid basis, such was the end which he so nearly attained.

* * * * *

by the battle of Marengo he obtained the peace which France so much required. But peace is of too short duration: England wishes to have war. It seems that the two most civilized nations are compelled by Providence to enlighten the world, the one by exciting the nations against France, the other by conquering and afterwards regenerating them. For a moment these two colossi look each other in the face---there is only a narrow strait to cross-they set to work and fight. But such is not their proper task. The genius of civilization should march towards the Ea.st.

* * * *

In 1812, the conflict becomes more terrible. In order that •niversal peace might be established, it was necessary that England on the west, and Russia on the east, should be persuaded by reason, or overcome in battle. The grand designs of the Emperor were nearly accomplished; the west of Europe marches upon Moscow. But, alas! a. winter has changed all! !•..•.. Europe, after Napoleon's plan, could no longer exist.

* * * *

WATERLOO !...... Here the voice of every Frenchman fails, he can only shed tears! tears to weep with the conquered, tears to weep with the conquerors, who will sooner or later regret having overthrown the only man who made himself a mediator between two hostile ages!

All our wars have come to us from England. Never has she been willing to entertain any proposition of peace. Did she then believe that the Emperor wished for her destruction? He never had such an idea. It was only a question of reprisals. The Emperor esteemed the English people, and he would have made every sacrifice to obtain pea.ce--every, except such as would have compromised his honour. In 1800, the First Consul wrote to the King of England : " Must the war, which for eight years has devastated the four quarters of the world, be eternal ! Are there no means by which we may come to an understanding! How is it that the two most enlightened nations of Europe, powerful and strong, even more than is enough to secure their safety and independence, can sacrifice to ideas of empty grandeur the well-being of commerce, internal prosperity, the happiness of their families ! How is it they do not perceive that peace is the first thing needful, as it is the first of things glorious !"

In 1805, the Emperor addresses the following words to the same sovereign : " The world is large enough to permit our two nations to dwell therein, and reason has sufficient power to let us find means to make all peaceable, if on both sides there is the desire to do so. Peace is the wish of my heart; but war has never been the reverse of glorious to me. I conjure your Majesty not to deny yourself the happiness of being the one to bring about peace."

In 1808, at Erfurth, Napoleon unites with Alexander to lead the British Cabinet to ideas of conciliation.

Lastly, in 1812, when the Emperor was at the apogee of his power, he once more made the same proposals to England. Always after a victory he asked for peace. Never has he consented to it after a defeat. " A nation," he said, " finds fresh men more easily than it recovers lost honour."

It would be too painful to think that the wa.r was prolonged only because of the hateful passions or interests of parties. If a struggle so desperate had such a lengthy duration, it is doubtless because the two peoples had too little knowledge of each other, and that each government was in error with respect to the condition of its neighbour. England, perhaps, saw in Napoleon only a despot oppressing his country, exhausting its resources to satisfy hie ambition as a warrior; she knew not how to believe that the Emperor was the elect of the people, and that he represented all the material and moral interests for which France had fought ever since 1789. In the same way it might be advanced that the French government, confounding the enlightened aristocracy of England with the feudal aristocracy which lay so heavily on France before the Revolution, believed that it had to deal with an oppressive government. But the aristocracy of England is like the Briareus of fable: it holds to the people by a hundred thousand roots : from the people it has obtained as many sacrifices as Napoleon obtained efforts from the French nation. And, what is worth remarking in the strife between these two countries, the rivalry of England put Napoleon in a position to realise against that power a European project similar to that which Henri IV. would have carried out against Spain, in concert with Elizabeth, if the dagger of an assassin had not torn away that great monarch from France and from Europe.

*　　　*　　　*　　　*

If war is the scourge of humanity, this scourge loses a large portion of its unhappy influence when force of arms is invoked to establish, instead of to destroy. The wars of the Empire have been like the overflow of the Nile : when the waters of this river cover the plains of Egypt, one might believe that there was nothing but dev~tation ; but they have scarcely returned to their channels when abundance and fertility spring up wherever the floods had extended !

CHAPTER V.

THE OBJECT WHICH THE EMPEROR HAD IN VIEW.

When the fate of battle had rendered Napoleon master of the greatest part of the Continent, he wished to use his conquests for the purpose of establishing a confederation of all Europe.

• • • •

To establish between the nations of Europe a social relation instead of a state of rude nature, such was the thought of the Emperor ; all his political combinations tended towards this immense result ; but to attain it, it was necessary to induce England and Russia frankly to second his wishes.

" As long as there is any fighting in Europe," said Napoleon, " it can be called nothing but civil war."

• • • •

Napoleon displaced sovereigns because, at the

time, it was for the interest of the peoples that he should do so; in 1815, the peoples were set aside for the particular benefit of the rulers. The statesmen of that period, consulting passions and animosities alone, based the balance of power in Europe on the rivalries of great powers, instead of establishing it on the basis of general interests ; therefore their system is everywhere crumbling a.way.

The policy of the Emperor, on the contrary, consisted in founding a solid European association, in making his system rely upon nationalities complete, and on the promotion of general interests. If fortune had not abandoned him, he would have had in his hands all the means necessary for setting Europe at rest : he had kept in reserve whole countries which he might have disposed of so as to can-y out his purpose.

● ● ● ●

European interests would have controlled national interests; humanity would have been satis--fied ; for Providence cannot have intended that :one nation should be happy only at the expense of others, and that in Europe there should be only conquerors and conquered, instead of reconciled members of one great family.

The greater the amount of moral force any authority has, the less necessary is it to make use of material appliances ; the more public opinion entrusts it with power, the better able is it to dispense with the exercise thereof.

●   ●   ●   ●

It is with a feeling like that left by an enchanting dream that one dwells upon the picture of happiness and stability which Europe would have presented had the vast projects of the Emperor been accomplished. Each country, confined within its natural bounds, united to its neighbour by the ties of interest and of friendship, would have enjoyed in its interior the benefits of independence, of peace and liberty. The sovereigns, exempt from fear and suspicion, would have applied themselves seriously to making better the condition of their peoples, and would have striven to bring home all the advantages of civilization.

Instead of that, what have we now in Europe? Every one as he falls asleep at night dreads the awakening of the morrow ; for the germ of evil is everywhere, and every honest soul almost doubts as to what is good, because of the sacrifices which its attainment would demand.

Men of liberty, who rejoiced over the fall of Napoleon, your error has been fatal! How many years must yet elapse, what combats and sacrifices must there be before you reach the point to which Napoleon had conducted you!

And you, statesmen of the Congress of Vienna, who were masters of the world, standing over the ruins of the Empire, how grand a *role* you might have played, but you comprehended it not! In the name of liberty, carried even to excess, you raised the peoples against Napoleon; you placed him under the ban of Europe as a despot and a tyrant! you declared that you had delivered the nations and secured their repose. They believed you at the moment; but nothing solid can be built upon a, lie and on a mistaken principle! Napoleon had closed the gulf of revolutions: you re-opened it by overthrowing him. Take care that the gulf does not close upon yourselves!

CHAPTER VI.

CAUSE OF THE EMPEROR'S FALL.

• • •   But, it will be said, the edifice which you hold to be so solid as to its internal principles, has been overthrown. The foreign policy which you consider so profound, was the very cause of his ruin!

To this we answer: The internal construction of the edifice was solid; for not from the interior came the shock which overturned it ; as to the system planned by the Emperor, it was not able to establish itself definitively, and for us to form a just estimate of its value, it must ha.ve been previously put into practice.

The Emperor fell because he too soon accomplished his work ; because events followed eaeb. other with too great rapidity ; he conquered, so to speak, too promptly.   His genius was far ahead of the men and the times; had he been fortunate, men would have esteemed him as a deity; unfortunate, people only think how rash he was. Carried on by the stream of victory, Napoleon could not be followed in his rapid flight by philosophers, who, confining their ideas within the narrow circle of the domestic hearth, for a single ray of liberty, helped to extinguish the very furnace of civilization.

On the other hand, foreign countries, impatient because of the evils of war pressing upon them for the time, forgot the benefits which Napoleon conferred upon them, and on account of a passing evil, they rejected the entire future of independence.

* * * *

Time not having cemented his alliances, nor effaced the remembrance of too recent animosities, at the very first check, his allies turned against him. Deceived in his expectations, the Emperor would no longer adhere to propositions which he did not believe to be sincere; foreigners, on their eide, when they saw that Napoleon was always more haughty after a defeat, thought that he never would consent to a definitive peace.

Napoleon fell only because his projects becoming

greater in proportion as the elements at his disposal were multiplied, he wished, in ten years of empire, to accomplish the work of several ages.

Not from lack of ability did the Emperor fall, but through exhaustion ; :nd, notwithstanding frightful reverses, calamities without number, the French people always strengthened his hands by their votes, sustained him by their efforts, encouraged him by their attachment.

It is a consolation for those who feel the blood of the great man flowing through their veins, to think of the regrets which followed his disappearance. A grand and proud thought it is that it required all the efforts of Europe combined to tear Napoleon away from that France which he had made so great ! It was not the people of France in their wrath who undermined his throne; twice it required 1,200,000 foreigners to break the Imperial sceptre!

Funeral procession suitable to the greatest sovereign, his country in tears, and glory in mourning attire go with him to his last resting-place !

THE NAPOLEONIAN IDEA.

THE NAPOLEONIAN IDEA.

[In 1840, Louis Napoleon published *l'Idle Napoleonienne* : this is the only number of a publication which it was intended should come out monthly, but no second number came to light. In August, 1840, the rash attempt at Boulogne ended in the arrest of L. Napoleon. He was condemed to perpetual imprisonment, and was sent to the fortress of Ham, where he remained till May, 1846, at which time he made bis escape, and took refuge in England.]

• • • •

The Napoleonian idea. sprang from the revolution as Minerva from the head of Jupiter : helmet on head, completely clothed in armour. It fought in order to exist, it triumphed only to persuade, it yielded to rise a.gain from its ashes, therein following a Divine example !

Napoleonism consists in reconstructing French

society ruined by fifty years of revolution, in reconciling order with liberty; the rights of the people with the principles of authority.

Standing between two infuriated parties, one of which sees nothing but the past, whilst the other looks only at the future, it adopts ancient forms, new principles.

Wishing to have a solid foundation, it bases its system on principles of eternal justice, and crushes beneath its feet the reactionary theories engendered by the excesses of parties.

It replaces the hereditary system of ancient aristocracies with one that is hierarchical, which, whilst it recognises equality, recompenses merit and guarantees order.

It finds an element of power and of stability in a democracy, because it disciplines the mass.

It finds an element of strength in liberty, because it wisely prepares its reign by establishing wide-spread foundations before constructing the edifice.

It follows neither the uncertain course of a party, nor the passions of the crowd: it commands through reason, it guides because it walks in advance.

Soaring above political coteries, exempt from all national prejudice, it sees in France only brothers who can easily be reconciled, and in the different nations of Europe only the members of one and a great family.

It proceeds not by exclusion, but by reconciliation ; it unites instead of dividing the nation. It gives to each the employment which is due to him, the place which he merits according to his capacity and his works, without demanding from any an account of his opinion, or of his political antecedents.

Attending only to the public weal, it does not seek out by what artificial measure it may sustain a tottering power, but by what means it can render the country prosperous.

It attaches importance to facts alone ; it abhors useless words. The measu~es which others have been discussing for ten years, it executes them in a single year. It careers with full sails over the ocean of civilization instead of remaining in a stagnant pond, uselessly making trial of every sort of sail.

It rejects the polemics of the day which are like the religious discussions of the middle ages, when they fought about metaphysical questions concerning the transubstantiation of the blood of our Lord, instead of enlarging upon the grand principles of the Gospel. Also it never raises its voice to blame, or to adopt a microscopic law relating to guarantees which are only imaginary, about reactionary exclusions, or mutilated franchises; it plays not with the toys of children, but, itself a giant, when it does fight, it is a war of Titans; its arms are entire peoples, and its triumphs or reverses are for the world the signal of slavery or of liberty.

Napoleouism divides itself into as many branches as the genius of man has varieties of phases; it tends to revive agriculture, it calls into being new productions, it borrows from foreign lands inventions which may be useful to its cause. It levels mountains, crosses rivers, facilitates communications, and compels the nations to shake hands.

It employs the arms of every one, and Intelligencies of every description. It enters the cottages of the poor, not holding out barren declarations of the rights of man, but with the means necessary to quench the poor man's thirst, to satisfy his hunger; and more than this, it recites a tale of glory to kindle his patriotic love. The Napoleonian idea is like the idea of the Gospel: it avoids luxury, and needs neither pomp nor ceremony, to make its own way, and secure a general reception ; only at the last extremity does it invoke the god of war. Humble without baseness, it knocks at every door, endures injury without returning hatred or rancour, and always marches unhesitatingly, because it knows that light precedes, and the peoples follow it.

The Napoleonian idea, conscious of its own strength, puts far away corruption, :flattery and falsehood-t.he vile auxiliaries of weakness. Although it expects everything at the hands of the people, it :flatters them not; it despises those democratic phrases by means of which it is attempted to gain paltry sympathies, after the fashion of the courtiers who enraged the great. king in his old age, by extolling him for merits which he no longer possessed. Its aim is not to create a passing popularity by reigniting hatreds imperfectly extinguished, and :flattering dangerous passions ; it apeaks its thoughts to every person, king or tribune, rich or poor; it praises oi blames, according as actions are praiseworthy or worthy of contempt.

The Napoleonian idea has loug since gained the sympathy of the ~s, because with the people sentiments are in advance of reasoning, the heart feels before the mind conceives. At the first preaching of Christianity, the nations adopted it before they understood the entire of its moral system. The influence of a great genius, therein resembling the Divine influence, is a fluid which spreads itself like electricity, exalts the imagination, makes men's hearts to beat, and carries them along because it moves the soul more than it exercises persuasion.

This influence, which it believes it exercises upon the mass, it would employ, not to overthrow society, but, on the contrary, to resettle and reorganise it. The Na.poleonian idea is, then, an idea of peace rather than an idea of war, an idea of order and of reconstruction, rather than an idea of overthrow. It professes without malice, and without hatred, the political moral which the great man was first to conceive. It develops the grand principles of justice, of authority, of liberty, too oft forgotten in these troublous times.

Wishing above all to persuade and convince, it preaches concord and confidence, and appeals to reason much more willingly than to force. But if, driven to extremity by too weat provocation, it should become the sole hope of unhappy populations, and the last refuge of the glory and honour of the land, then, resuming its helmet and its spear, and mounting the altar of its country, it would say to the people, deceived by so many ministers and orators, that which saint Remi said to the proud Sicambre : " Throw down your false gods and your images of clay: burn what you have hitherto adored, and worship that which you have lately burnt."

ANSWER TO M. DE LAMARTINE.

[M. de Lamartine, writing to M. Chapuys-Montlaville, deputy, made use of expressions relating to the consulate and the empire which called forth an answer from L. Napoleon. The prisoner of Ham addresses his remarks to M. Chapuys-Montlaville; dated from the fortress of Ham, August 23, 1843.j

* * * *

Another complaint : " Napoleon everywhere in Europe extinguishes the love and peaceful propagation of French ideas." Why, when General Bonaparte took the helm of affairs, the Republic was at war with the whole of Europe ; all foreign peoples, without exception, were exasperated against France; the magnificent truths proclaimed by our national assemblies had been obscured by so many passions, that they were misunderstood ! Where, then, was to be found that *peaceful propagation* to which M. de Lamartine refers ? On the contrary, Napoleon it was, who, arresting the stream of passions, everywhere secured the triumph of the truths of the French revolution. He it was who implanted in Poland, in Italy, in Germany, in Spain, in Switzerland, the ideas and civilizing laws of France. Who does not know that in Germany he, with a single stroke of his pen, erased two hundred and forty-three small feudal States; that from the Vistula to the Rhine he destroyed bondage, feudal abuses, and introduced there the French civil code, publicity of trial by jury in criminal cases, tore up by the roots religious animosities, and there established freedom of worship ! Who does not know that in Poland, in Italy, he created powerful germs of nationality, raised national tribunes, and everywhere spread the benefits of enlightened government ? Who does not know that in Switzerland he made peace between the Cantons, and gave them a federal compact, the loss of which they at this day are lamenting? Lastly, who does not know that in Spain even he destroyed the Inquisition, the feudal system, and made every effort to establish a constitution more liberal, and a government more enlightened than all those which we have seen there during the last twenty-eight years! Later still, Coblentz, lighting up its walls because Prussia had not succeeded in wresting from her her French laws, rendered splendid homage to the Emperor's memory.

"The result of the Empire," says the illustrious writer whom I refute with pain, " is Europe twice in Paris, England realizing without a rival universal supremacy over the sea; in France, reason, liberty, and the condition of the mass retarded by this period of glory." It is true in this sense that the disastrous results came, not from the triumph, but *from tke fall* of the Emperor. Mourn, therefore, with us, with France, with the peoples, over the reverses which befell our arms; for if they had always been victorious to the end, England would have been humbled, the oligarchy of Europe conquered, the nationalities of neighbouring peoples resuscitated, liberty at last implanted in Europe !

I do not systematically defend all the institutions of the Empire nor all the actions of the Emperor: I explain them. I regret the creation of a nobility which, from the very day after the fall of its originator, has forgotten its plebeian origin to make common cause with the oppressors; I regret certain acts of violence useless for the maintenance of a power which was based upon the wish of the. people: but what I do assert is that, of all governments which preceded or followed the Consulate and the Empire, not one did, even in time of peace, for the prosperity of France, the thousandth part of what the Emperor effected during a wide-spread war.

● ● ● ●

Consul, he established in France the chief benefits of the revolution: emperor, he spread the same benefits throughout the whole of Europe. His mission, at first exclusively French, afterwards embraced the whole human race.

* * * *

Eh! how is this! M. de Lamartine can find regrets and tears for the violences of the minister Polignac, but his eye remains dry and his language is bitter when he sees our eagles falling at Waterloo, and our plebeian Emperor dying at Saint Helena!

* * * *

POLITICAL REVERIES.

[Political Reveries were written in 1832: M. de Ohateaubriand was at that time in Switzerland: the Prince submitted his work to him, asking for suggestions.]

• • • •

The first requirements of a country are independence, liberty, stability, the supremacy of merit, and an equally-spread state of comfort. That government will be the best where every abuse of power can always be corrected, where, without social disorder, without bloodshed, the laws and the head of the State can at any time be changed, for one generation cannot subject to its own laws the generations which follow.

That *independence* ma.y be certain, it is necessary that the government be strong, and, that it may be strong, it must have the confidence of the people, it must be able to have at its command a large and well-disciplined army without calling forth an outcry against tyranny, it must be able to ann the whole nation without having to dread its own overthrow.

To be free, which is only a consequence of independence, it is necessary that the whole people, without distinction, shall be able to vote at elections of the representatives of the nation; it is requisite that the mass, which cannot be corrupted, and which neither flatters nor dissembles, shall be the constant source whence power is derived.

• • • •

According to the opinions which I advance, it will be seen that my principles are entirely republican. Ah ! what pleasanter, indeed, than to dream about the empire of virtue, the development of our faculties, the progress of civilization? If, in my plan of a constitution, I give preference to the monarchical form, it is because I think that such a government is more suited to France, inasmuch as it would give more guarantees for a state of tranquillity, of authority, and liberty.

If the Rhine were a sea, if virtue were always the only moving power, if merit alone rose to govern, then I would have a republic pure and simple.

•

Harmony between the government and the governed can exist in two ways only: when the people permits itself to be governed by the will of a single individual, or when the chief governs in accordance with the wishes of all. In the first ease, it is despotism; in the second, it is liberty. The tranquillity of the one is the silence of the tomb; the tranquillity of the other is the serenity of a pure sky.

People talk of eternal conflicts, of interminable strifes, and yet it would be easy for sovereigns to consolidate peace that would last for ever: let them consult the relations and the manners of different nations between themselves, let them give to them their nationalities and the institutions which they ask for, and they will have found the true balance of power. Then all the peoples will be brothers, and will embrace each other in the sight of tyranny dethroned, of the earth consoled, and of humanity satisfied.

THE CONSERVATIVE PARTY.

Since 1815, we have been condemned to copy in everything our neighbours on the other side of the Channel. If imitation always secured resemblance, our advice would be to persist in this imitation with perseverance, for in England there are beautiful and grand institutions. But, unfortunately, servile copies never have other than a pernicious result. Let us take our neighbour's coat, if you absolutely insist upon it, but at any rate let us cut it so as to suit our own figure.

Let us make use of the experience of the English to transplant into our land analogous laws; but let us not adopt their parliamentary language, nor their party denominations, for wa should no longer be able to understand each other.

We have neither the same character, nor the same manners, nor the same nature : the same words would represent two things totally opposed to each other.

However, there is in France a political fraction which gives itself the pompous title of Conservative ! Is it not ridiculous to call themselves thus in a country where nothing is where it should be, and where everything ought to be changed] In England, on the contrary, one can easily understand this party denomination, because society reposes up_on bases which have endured through ages.

We do not agree with the opinions of the Tory party, but we admit that it might say to the English people : " ,Ve call ourselves Conservatives because we. wish to preserve a political system which has made England to be one of the first powers of the world; because with this system, perseveringly followed during more than a century, we have covered the land with works of every description, raised our industry and our commerce to the highest degree, and carried the glory of our arms from one end of the world to the other ; we are proud of our ancient system, because we have governed all the time maintaining individual liberty and freedom of the press, because we have served but one dynasty, taken but one oath, and never made common cause with the enemy of our country. We are proud of our past history, we have doubts as to the future ; that is the reason why we are Conservatives."

   *   *   *   *

As to our relations with the foreigner, on that point still less can be said in explanation of a Conservative system. Our representatives are only just tolerated in the courts of the north ; in south ern courts they are without influence. In the north as in the south, our policy is as contradictory as it is uncertain , in the east as in the west no one knows what we wish; indeed, it is doubted whether we are capable of wishing at all. In fact, nowhere do we command respect, nowhere do we receive sympathy; we should be the laughing-.stock of Europe, and the neighbouring powers would despise us, if they were able to forget what we have been in former days.

   •   •   •

PERSONAL FREEDOM IN ENGLAND.

In general, it is correct to say that there is more freedom in England and greater equality in France. This results from the different organizations of the two societies. In those countries where there exists a powerful aristocracy, the great families were always zealous defenders of freedom, because they stood in nefd of it for themselves, as a guarantee against the power of the monarch, whilst they always arrayed themselves against any approach to equality, because it attacks their own privileges.

[The writer then proceeds to the Magna Charta wrested from King John in 12M; to the Petition of Right in the third year of the reign of Charles I.; to the definitive vote of the Habeas Corpus. in the 31st year of the reign of Charles IL (Charles II. reckoned the years of exile as years of his reign.) The statute of Habeas Corpus principally applied to those who were accused of criminal misdoings; but, by another statute, in 1816, it was extended to all cases of illegal detention.]

There is no public accuser in England, for the attorney-general interferes only in extraordinary cases. There is no doubt but that many guilty persons escape justice through the want of such a. functionary ; but, again, personal liberty runs less chance of being violated.

But it is not the laws only which protect the citizens, it is also the manner in which they are executed, it is the way in which the government exercises its power. In England, authority never ir,,; exerted in a passionate spirit : its proceedings are moderate, and always in accordance with law ; therefore, such a thing is never heard of as violation of a, citizen's house, a proceeding rathe.r common in France, under the name of domiciliary visits ; family secrets are respected, because correspondence is never subjected to inspection; no restraint is mid upon that first of all liberties, the right to go wherever you like, for no one is required to have a passport, an invention injurious to the well-being of the public, for it is an encumbrance and an obstacle to a. peaceful citizen, without checking, in any way whatever, those who wish to avoid the vigilance of the authorities.

Another guarantee of liberty is the organization

of the police, for, instead of provoking in order to punish, this body prevents the commission of crime, and thus diminishes the number of punishments.

• • • •

The accused can appeal to a power which has never failed in England when it has been invoked for the protection of liberty : that power is public opinion.

* • • •

In France, where people are so jealous of anything which concerns equality and the national honour, there is no strong conscientious regard for the liberty of the individual. You may trouble the tranquillity of her citizens, you may violate their homes, you may make them undergo during entire months a precautionary imprisonment, you may despise personal securities, a few generous men will raise their voices, but public opinion will remain ealm and unmoved, so long as you do not rouse any political passion.

Therein lies the great cause of the violence of power: it can be arbitrary, because it finds no restraint. In England, on the .contrary, political passions subside when there is a violation of a common right. This is because England is a country which respects the law, whilst France has been fighting for the last forty years, alternating between revolutions and counter-revolutions, and because a high-minded observance of principles has yet to be created there.

THE SLAVE TRADE.

PHILANTHROPISTS AND THE RIQHT OF SEARCH.

Let us honour philanthropists who, by a happy application of a lofty idea of philosophy, promote the well-being of their fellow-creatures ; but let us be on our guard against those men who proclaim theories more brilliant than true, who follow up an idea without troubling themselves as to the contrary effects which it produces, and who, although they wish to include all the world in their loving embrace, entail much misery on the human race. The particular character of those imperfect minds about which we would speak, consists in feeling passionately for troubles to which they are the greatest strangers, and which they know the least about. The ardour of men of this stamp always increases in direct proportion to the square of the distance at which the objects of their sympathy are to be found. They are insensible to the misery of the Frenchman of low degree, to the nakedness of the workman who lives under the same roof with themselves; but as soon as ever some iniquities are committed at our antipodes, oh! then their passions exalt themselves, humanity suffering at the end of the world appears to them much more worthy of pity than that which languishes in their own country. But, if in reality they did any good to any one, we would bless their efforts, for all men are brethren. Unfortunately, the entire opposite of this happens.

Let us come to the subject. Public feeling is roused in Europe against slavery and the slave trade. This sentiment was truthful, for it was of the people••·... But self-styled philosophers have taken possession of it, and have aggravated the evil they designed to cure. This is easily proved. In the greater part of the torrid countries of America, the soil is tilled exclusively by negroes. The African race is necessary to this climate : a state of slavery compelled it to labour, the trade each year augmented its number. The property of two-thirds of America depended upon slavery and the slave trade. A religious and Christian sentiment, which we are far from blaming, for we feel it ourselves, seized upon Europe; and, grieving over the sufferings of an entire race of men, it cried aloud: "No more slavery! no more slave-trade !" At these words the inhabitants of both Americas who are of European descent, replied to us : " Emancipation is with us only another tenn for theft, ruin, murder, for the slaves are. our property; we paid for them, if you free them you must buy them from us ; and, if you liberate them all at once, they *will* kill us. We also are your brethren, and we have a right to your protection,"

As this consideration was not wanting in justice, the French government answered: " Eh, well! eontinue your slavery until further orders ; but no more trade. We are about to put a stop to it by the treaty of the right of search." And, what has happened! This, the trade being for many parts of America an imperious necessity, as long as slavery existed, it was sure to be persevered in ; and so it is carried on as a contraband traffic on just as large a scale. So long as the market remained)pen, it was impossible openly to prohibit sales ; so long as a society feels anything to be an imperi-)us necessity, it always finds the means for satisfying that want. The poor negroes, instead of being crammed in vessels by twenties are stuffed into them by hundreds, and, when the vessels which carry them are pursued by philanthropical cruisers, the commanders hurl them into the sea to save themselves from the penalties imposed by the governments of Europe. We may cite, in proof of what we advance, one fact taken from a hundred, which occurred on the coast of Brazil, in *1886,* and which was known to the whole French squadron.

An English cruiser perceives a ship whose proceedings seem to it to be those of a slaver ; it puts itself in pursuit of the ship. The latter makes off with all sails set. However, the English corvette follows close, it is just on the point of coming up with it, when it perceives that the ship is disencumbering itself of a great quantity of barrels, which it casts into the sea. One of these barrels happens to float close to the English vessel ; it is seized, it is ta.ken on board, it is opened ; a cry of horror escapes from the mouths of the sailors : a negro is enclosed in the cask, and the same with others which are recovered from the sea. The slaver wished, by this device, to conceal the nature of his cargo; the laws of philanthropists have changed a seller of slaves into an assassin! and this is not an isolated case. It is asserted that Brazil receives more negroes annually as contraband, than it received previous to the treaties for the suppression of traffic in human beings. In this way, therefore, negroes suffer much greater tortures than in former times; the right of search has been of no use- to the cause of humanity, and as long as slavery exists, it will be the same.

What is to be done in the matter! This: Had the grand question of the abolition of slavery been conducted by governments, by men sincerely wishing the good of humanity, that is to say, the prosperity of the white race and of the black race, they would first have accustomed the slaves of their own colonies, by causing them gradually to undergo an apprenticeship, to pass insensibly from forced to free labour. During this time they would, in concert with all governments which countenance slavery, have taken care that the trade was carried on with humanity, by inflicting severe punishment on every captain of a ship who had not given to his negroes the same accommodation which is farnished to Europeans emigrating to America. All the governments of Europe should have come to a mutual understanding to persuade the governments of America to follow their example, and then their word would have carried weight, whilst do-day the ..8.razilian Government, for example, can demand of France by what right she prevents the importation of slaves, since she herself has slaves in her own colonies.

When once slavery had been abolished, the trade evidently would have been abolished by the same stroke, and the laws of humanity would have been satisfied. Whilst at this day hatred has been raised between the master and the slave, the trade is carried on as contra.band and becomes more atrocious, in proportion to the increased wish to repress it. In short, it 'serves as a pretext for English vengeance, for England is ready to make war, that is to say, to cause the deaths of thousands of Englishmen and Frenchmen, in this pretended interest of humanity.

Let us repeat, therefore, in conclusion, that if' philanthropy which sees correctly and well is one of the most beautiful of human virtues, false philanthropy is the worst of all mistakes ; and here we call to mind the remarkable words of M. Villemain, at a time when he wa.s not minister: "It must be that truth is a thing very precious in itself, since the generous errors of pure minds are almost as fatal to humanity as crime, which is an error of wicked men."-*Progr~a du Paa-de-Calais, Feb.* 4, 1843.

OPINION OF THE EMPEROR

ON THE

RELATIONS BETWEEN FRANCE AND THE POWERS OF EUROPE.

Polemics have been devoted, for the last twelve years, to showing alternately the advantages of an alliance with England, or an alliance with Russia, as though it were absolutely necessary that France should intimately connect herself with one or other of these two great powers. According to these two discussions which resound through the political world, it would appear that France has need of some strength other than her own to cause her to be respected, of another voice besides her own, to secure a hearing in the congress of kings. We do not wish to assert that she ought to remain isolated, and have no frank and friendly relations with any power; but we believe that an alliance should be the result of protracted kind intercourse between nations, and not the fruit of a sudden impulse. Here are the words of the Emperor Napoleon :-

" France is, by her geographical situation, the richness of her soil, and the intelligent energy of her inhabitants, the arbiter of European society ; she steps out of the *rok* which nature assigns her when she becomes a conqueror ; she fails in it when she obeys the obligations of any alliance whatsoever. She is to the nations of Europe what the lion is to the animals which surround him. She cannot move without being either a protector or a destroyer · she lends the aid of her power, but she never exchanges it, in her own interest, for any help that can be necessary for her own defence. Her own power is always sufficient for her, even when she finds herself for the time being weakened by that sickness of nations-internal divisions. For she requires but one convulsive effort to punish her enemies for having dared to challenge her to fight.

" In 1793, the whole of Europe coalesced against' France ; a hundred thousand men of La Vendee, subsidized by England, threatened Paris : one million three hundred thousand Frenchmen enlisted for love of their country, and not, as people have been heard to say, to escape the axe of the lictors of a Robespierre or a Couthon. The coalition was vanquished, condemned to recognize the Republic.

" What France did at that time, she was able to do in 1814 and 1815; her comparative exhaustion was more than compensated by the advantages of her unity, of her obedience to the order of one ma.n; neither the occupation of Paris, nor the battle of Waterloo condemned her to pass under *thecaudine forl»,* Bonaparte as a general would have saved it, as an Emperor he lost it by abdicating.

"\Vhen we have the honour and the happiness to belong to France, we should understand all the responsibility of such a favoured position; and, from the sun-nation which it is, not allow it to be changed into a satellite-nation.

"England, all-powerful as she is, cannot by herself interfere in the affairs of the Continent and play the first *role;* she must, from sheer necessity, lean upon Vienna, Paris, or Saint Petersburgh, and, aware of this, Lord Castlereagh decorated with the pompous title of kingdom the territories of Hanover, in order to secure a royal antry into the Germanic diet."

What has happened during the last twelve years proves the truth and the depth of Napoleon's opinion. In 1830, the French Government warmly solicited the acknowledgment and alliance of England, and England answered: " We will defend your ideas in the face of Europe ; but hand over to us your interests. Recognize the treaties of 1815 and the supremacy of our navy, bind yourselves to evacuate Algeria whenever we may demand it, to sacrifice to us even some of your industrial resources, and to permit our influence to be established in the East and in the Mediterranean." These promises having been made, England demands, when she thinks it is a favourable moment, the execution of the engagements entered into. She is exercising only her right ; but why has our government, through its own chief, promised away our future, and for the interest of a dynasty abandoned the great interests of the country ? We are desirous that a good intelligence shall exist between the two most civilized people of the globe ; but on condition that the rights and the dignity of each shall have been weighed with the same weight8 in the same balance, and that the men charged with the high mission of securing peace between two rival peoples shall have no other aim than the welfare of France and the development of her agricultural, industrial, and commercial riches : development which takes place only when men follow a policy which is frank, energetic, national. --{Progr~s du Paa-de-Calais, 22 March, 1843.)

HISTORICAL FRAGMENTS

1688 AND 1830.

PREFACE.

In presenting to the public this extract from my historical studies I yield to the desire of repelling unjust attacks, by the simple exposition of my convictions and thoughts.

I am not ignorant that silence accords well with misfortune ; it is useless for the vanquished to fight over again with fortune the trial to which he has been subjected by man. However, when the conquerors have abused their victory so far as to have revenged themselves upon me as though they had been defeated, calling to their aid those weapons of weakness and fear, calumny and falsehood, resistance becomes a duty, and silence would be cowardice.

Far be from me the thought of recommencing a controversy, where the passions always wrestle with more success than reason ! It suffices me, to avenge my honour, to prove that if I have embarked boldly on a stormy sea, it is not without having beforehand profoundly meditated on the causes and effects of revolutions, on the dangers attending success, as well as on the whirlpools which swallow the wreck. Whilst in Paris they deify the mortal remains of the Emperor, I, his nephew, am interred alive in a narrow space; but I laugh at the inconsistency of man, and I thank Heaven for having given me as a refuge, after so many grievous trials, a prison on the soil of France. Sustained by an ardent faith and a pure conscience, I envelope myself in my misfortune with resignation, and I console myself for the present in contemplating the future of my enemies written in ineffaceable characters in the history of all nations.

NAPOLEON LOUIS BONAPARTE.

Castle of Ham, May 10, 1841.

CHAPTER I.

INTRODUCTION.

In the year 1649, England was convulsed by a great revolution : the head of a king rolled upon the scaffold; the Republic was proclaimed, and it lasted eleven years. [1]

In 1660, the son of the beheaded monarch was brought back in triumph to London.

Charles II. reigned a quarter of a century ; but in 1685 he left his brother a tottering sovereignty, which James II. was able to maintain for three years only. At length, in 1688, a fresh revolution established itself as mediator between all the parties which had been dividing England for forty-eight years.

[1] The Republic was proclaimed in 1649; the Protectorsbip was established in 1653; Cromwell died in 1658; and two years after his death the Restoration took place.

In France also we have experienced a revolution which has overturned its ancient government ; a scaffold, a republic, an empire, a restoration, and a new revolution; but will the year 1830, like the year 1688, be turned to by future generations, as the commencement of a new era of glory and liberty ! Such is the question which interests us all.

It would be easy for us to reject at once the comparison of events which occurred in the two countries, and to show that it is only in the skeletons of the two histories that a resemblance is to be found. It would be easy for us to prove that at the commencement of both the first revolutions, English society was very different from the society of France. It would be easy for us to prove that the Empire, an imperishable ~onument of civil and military glory, resembles in no respect the bloody and fanatical power of Cromwell, and :finally that the restoration of the Bourbons differs, in many respects, from the restoration of the Stuarts. But after the example of many commendable writers, we will pass over all these dissimilarities, and will for a moment admit a resemblance in the last two epochs, for the purpose of considering whether the causes which consolidated the revolution of 1688 will also consolidate the revolution of 1830.

The life of a people is composed of dramas perfect in themselves, and of isolated acts. When we view at a glance the entire scope of the drama, we discover the reason of all its actions, the connexion between ideas, and the cause of every change ; but if we consider only the separate acts, these great social convulsions then no longer appear anything more than the effects of chance and human inconsistency.

In bringing together the detached periods of the history of Great Britain, without considering their philosophical affinity, we see the people of England adoring the absolute power of Elizabeth, and overturning the less arbitrary power of Charles I. We see them in revolt against this prince for levying a few illegal imposts, and then suffering themselves immediately after to be taxed and governed, without control or legal right,[1] by the Long Parliament of Cromwell. We see them at length, by their own free choice, at the feet of Charles II.

[1] We say *legal right* because the Long Parliament of Cromwell had not legitimatized its power by a free election.

abjuring the revolution, only to find them later cursing his rule, and overthrowing his brother.

What contradictions does not this superficial view of facts appear to contain! And yet, if we embrace with a glance the whole historic drama which commenced in the sixteenth century, the development of which took place only at the end of the seventeenth century, we shall see that the English nation has always willed the same thing, and that it never rested until it had attained the object of its wishes and the aim of its desires.

Ever since the sixteenth century, the English have endeavoured to obtain :

First, and before all things, the firm establishment of their reformed religion, which with them represented all the interests of the nation.

Secondly, the preponderance of their navy, by means of which they increase their influence on the continent.

Thirdly, the complete exercise of their liberties.

Elizabeth assured the triumph of the Protestant cause, she increased the glory of the nation. Her memory was blessed.

The republic and Cromwell concealed, beneath the shelter of the national dignity, their despotic and exclusive policy. They passed away. The Stuarts spurned equally the three great objects of desire which engaged the hearts of the majority of the English. They fell.

William III. alone established at the same time the religion, the glory, and the liberty of his country. He consolidated his work.

Therefore, it is not chance that rules the fate of nations; it is no unforeseen accident that overturns or maintains thrones ; there is one general cause that rules events, and makes them logically depend upon each other. A government may often violate the laws or even liberty with impunity ; but, if it does not freely put itself at the head of the grand interests of civilization, it has but an ephemeral duration ; and this simple philosophical cause, which occasions its death, is *called fatality*, because we do not choose to account for its existence.

To attribute the fall of empires to secondary events, is to take for the *cause* of danger that which only served to make it known.

England required almost an entire age during which society struggled with the evil passions of power, and power struggled with the evil passions of society, to build the immense English fabric which we have hated, which we have endeavoured to overturn, but which it is impossible for us not to admire.

The national cause had these opposite obstacles to surmount, because it divided as soon as it was no longer led by the lofty spirit which animated Elizabeth; and sometimes it was betrayed by tyranny, which is the error of vice; sometimes mislead by fanaticism, which is the error of virtue.

In all countries, the wants and the grievances of people form themselves into ideas, into principles, the whence spring parties. Those associations of individuals, which spring from a common movement, but are composed of different spirits, have each their defects and their passions, as they have also each their truth. Compelled to act by the social fermentation, they strike and destroy themselves reciprocally, until national truth, forming itself out of all these partial truths, becomes raised, by common accord, above the reach of political passions.

To consolidate this cause, power must have a representative, having no interest other than its own.

Without doubt, for England, with its antecedents and its organization, the revolution of 1688 was, at the end of the seventeenth century, the sincere expression of this national truth, and William III. its veritable representative. The proof of this is, that, up to our own time, this revolu-'tion has given to England one hundred and fifty-three years of prosperity, grandeur, and liberty.

Will the revolution of July give to France the same advantages? It is for the future to resolve this question. For our part, without wishing to pierce into the secrets of Providence, let us content ourselves with examining the causes and effects of these grand political dramas, and let us seek in the history of the past some consolation for our misfortunes, some hope for our country.

CHAPTER II.

REVOLUTION OF]688. JAMES II.-WILLUM   III.

Like all countries which have been worked upon by successive revolutions, England, under James II., was given up to doubt and depression; all its characters seemed to be worn out, all its principles confused. How could it be otherwise, when, in less than fifty years, they had so often changed systems, without remedying the evils of society -

In 1640, the Parliament had admitted on principle that the nation could defend its rights against the enterprises of the king; in 1649, it had recognised the fact, that sovereign power resided in the nation alone; and in 1661, it had decided that power lay exclusively and entirely in the hands of the king.

The first declaration had brought about a revolution; the second, an usurpation; the third, a tyranny.

HISTORICAL FRAGMENTS. 79

Public spirit fluctuated uncertainly between all these remembrances, which reminded them how much the impetus had exceeded the mark.

Wearied with civil wars, disabused alike of the mysticism of parties and of the excellence of royal power, England had preserved from these struggles only one hatred and one love: hatred of popery and love of its own power.[1]

[1] In tracing the principal acts of the revolutions of England, one experiences at first a natural repugnance, when one is born a Catholic, to treat with contempt the men who sustained this religion in Great Britain; but, on examining the subject more closely, we see it is just to award it to those men who, by a blind zeal and by inconsiderate conduct, compromised and rendered unpopular, in 9England, the true doctrine of Christ, by making it a question of party, and a weapon for their passions. Their conduct deserves to be branded ; for never did the Catholic religion find itself in so favourable a position as in England, for ruling by the purity of its principles and the influence of its morals. Persecuted by regal power, it should have followed the example of the aristocracy, and have avenged itself for its oppression by putting itself at the head of the national liberties. Her position was admirable for acting thus, because she was independent of temporal power, acknowledging as head only the head of the universal Church, whilst the Anglicans held their rights and their powers only from the right and power of the head of the State; but, blinded by worldly interest,

In whom could she put confidence, when, in the space of an ordinary human life, she had been deceived by all whom she had loved - The Long Parliament had usurped her rights, and engendered a civil war; the Presbyterians had been as intolerant as the Catholics and as the Anglicans ; they were unable to foresee anything, or to establish anything. The Independents had produced only military despotism and anarchy.

The king had brought back with him from exile, only a reactionary and despotic spirit. In short, the Catholic clergy lost itself by making common cause with the oppressors of hie people, instead of uniting itself with the oppressed. Every enlightened spirit saw so clearly that the Stuarts ruined the cause of their religion, that Pope Innocent XI. loudly testified his displeasure at the imprudent conduct of James II., and the Cardinals of Rome said jokingly "that it would be necessary to excommunicate James II. as a man who was about to destroy the small amount of Catholicism that remained in England." But that which is not less remarkable is, that the Prince of Orange, head of the Protestant league, united in his favour, against a Catholic Sovereign, the Pope, Spain, and the Emperor of Germany; this proves that men ally themselves always with a cause which is nobly and frankly defended, whilst they desert even a friendly cause, when. it Is conducted by folly and cowardice.

the people put faith, under Charles II., in the patriotism of the chiefs of the parliamentary opposition, and these chiefs were most of them ambitious men, without conviction, or else sold to the foreigner.[1]

Doubt necessarily then reigned in men~s minds, and the nation preferred resigning itself to the chance of events, rather than run the risk of again deceiving itself by creating them itself; it is this which explains the almost universal acclamations which greeted the accession of James II.; they forgot the objections which existed during the preceding reign against the Duke of York, because it was more easy for dispirited minds to forget than to hate; and they began to hope from lassitude, as they had before hoped from enthusiasm.

James II. did not fail to lavish promises which were likely to flatter the national sentiment.

"I have," said the king in his first harangue, "' once hazarded my life for the defence of the nation, and I am as ready as any one to expose

---

[1] The despatches of Barillon prove that a great number of the members of the English Parliament received presents or money from France.· Hume cites the names of sixteen amons them. Vol. x., p. 55.

G

myself again to preserve to it its just rights and its liberties, ₁

" It was repeated everywhere in 1685 : We have now a king full of valour and dignity, who is going to make the nation respected abroad, who is going to raise it to the highest degree of glory and power, and who above all will know how best to oppose himself to the pretensions of Louis XIV., and to humble his pride." ₁ But James II. was one of those who precipitate catastrophes instead of retarding them. During his exile, he had abjured the religion of his fathers : and all his ideas, all his convictions were opposed to those of the English people. He found himself under the necessity of becoming perjured towards the nation or towards himself, and that community of sentiments which engenders eonfidenee not existing between them, dissimulation and violence became the sole support of his authority.

The first act of James II. was to demand subsidies from a foreign king; ¹ he violated his ~

₁ Hume, vol. x., p. 263..

₅ Boulay (de la Meurthe), *Hist~•* *Jqus* *11.*, t. i., p. ɔ.

³ Mazure, *Histoin ,k le Rlvol.tioa* de 1688, *i.* L, p. a.

mises, committed arbitrary acts, openly favoured the Catholic religion, and only made use of the Parliament to cover with a mantle of legality his tyrannical designs.

The Duke of Monmouth, the natural son of Charles II., knew the public mind, and was beloved by the people; a considerable party even wished to recognize in him the heir to the crown, to the injury of the Duke of York.

Exiled in the Low Countries, the Duke of Monmouth believed that he ought not to leave to James II. time for accomplishing his projects destructive of liberty, and resolved to overthrow him as early as the first year of his reign.

Confident in his courage and in the goodness of his cause, he landed at Lyme, in Dorsetshire, followed only by eighty-two men. As soon as the people had knowledge of his proclamations, they ran in crowds to join his standard, and already his army amounted to several thousand men, when it was put to the rout at Sedgemore; he himself was made prisoner, and was conducted to London and executed.

James II., alarmed at the danger of an expedition which had so nearly succeeded in raising the whole country against himself, did not content himself with striking the vanquished with all the severity of the laws, he would still further avenge himself by circulating such reports against the unfortunate Duke as would serve most to taint his memory.[1]

It was too much, however, to wrest from him at once his life and his honour; but nothing tends more to irritate an unpopular power than to see that a vanquished enemy is still a danger.

The enterprize of the Duke of Monmouth promised much to all the interests of the English people; why, then, did it not succeed? Was it irrevocably written in the destinies of England, that twenty-eight years should glide away after the Restoration before a national government should he able to establish itself? Had not twenty-five years sufficed to give fresh strength to its creeds, and to reanimate its courage? Nevertheless, the death of the Duke of Monmouth was not useless; he had opened the road along which, three years later, William was to march. The repression of thia

[1] In a despatch from Barillon, ambassador of France, t.o Louis XIV., it is stated as follows: "The court causes to be circulated all that can soil the memory of the Duke of Monmouth in the hearts of the Anglicans and the people."- Ma.zure, *Histoire de la Revolution de* 1688, t. ii., p. 9.

revolt and the attempt of the Earl of Argyll, which had occurred some time before in Scotland, tended only to augment the blindness and the boaBting of James. The most fatal gift which Providence can make to a government which is struggling against the national spirit, is to grant it ~asy victories; its triumph intoxicates it, and it takes for a symptom of its own strength that which is only a passing favour of fortune.

James II. wished to reign as men fight, by making sometimes false attacks, sometimes false retreats, in order to fall on his enemies, who were his subjects, when he believed that he had succeeded in dividing them. To accomplish his culpable projects, he called to his aid by turns despotism and liberty ; but, public opinion never following him in his enterprises, he could not gain credit for the possession of power or of a tolerant spirit. Opposition shortly manifested itself in the Chambers, amongst the nobility and amongst the clergy. Like all powers on the wane, he desired to replace moral force, which was abandoning him, by material force, and he now rested only on the counsels of a foreign ambassador and on his own standing army, which he had raised to the immense number for England of forty thousand men.'

But the army is a sword which has glory for its hilt; James II. could not wield it. England saw with anxiety the imprudent steps of the king, who trampled under foot its liberties, its religion, its municipal and university privileges, and who at the same time abandoned its glory and influence abroad. However, all remained in order, so great in unhealthy societies is that force of inertia which resists change.

The people shed many tears for those who foll in their enterprises against the government; and had great acclamations and cries of joy for those who, by acquittal of jury, escaped from the vengeance of power;[2] but they were too fatigued and too much divided to help themselves.

England was then about to perish ! So much blood shed for liberty, so many generous efforts to insure the progress of civilization-were these to end only in depotism and shame? They felt that such a result was impossible, without, however,

[1] Mazure, *Histoire de la Revolution de* 1688,t. iii.,p. 134.
[2] Acquittal of the bishops; popularity of the accused men of the Berwick regiment.

divining from what quarter salvation would come. They did not remain long without perceiving this. There lived a man in Holland, who, at the age of twenty-two yea.rs, had protected his country against the united fleets of France and England, against the armies commanded by Turenne, by Conde, by Luxembourg, by Vauban, and who had saved it by the unassisted energy of his spirit. Whilst every one despaired of the preservation of the ITnited Provinces, he alone, reckoning on the devotion of the people, had replied to the foreign ambassadors; who offered him shameful terms of peace: "I will defend my country to my last sigh, and I will die in the last intrenchment." William, Prince of Orange, was the head of the Protestant league in Europe; he had then a double title to the admiration of the English, his character and his religion.

Since his marriage with the eldest daughter of James II., then Duke of York, he had taken a lively interest in all that related to Great Britain. The deeds which passed before his eyes every day told him plainly what was his duty, and what it was that England expected of him. Penetrated by a deep conviction, which alone can inspire great actions, he resolved to make a descent upon this country, and to deliver it from the yoke that oppressed it.

What, under such grave circumstances, were the reasons which decided him in attempting an enterprize so perilous to his glory had it not succeeded ! Personal ambition, those will reply who desire incessantly to undervalue acts of great self-devotion, imputing to men only vulgar sentiments and sordid passions. No, the loftiest thoughts preside over great actions. William, surely, said to himself: I represent on the Continent the Protestant cause, which rests on liberty ; this cause has on its side the majority of the English nation. Oppressed, I will go and defend it. At the head of a few troops, I will pass the Channel in spite of the fleets of Louis XIV., and I will present myself to England as her liberator. The revolution which I will work by means of my army will have this advantage, that, without danger to the repose of the country, the wish of the nation will be able freely to manifest itself; for I shall have the power to restrain all the evil passions which ever rise high in political convulsions. I shall overturn a government whilst I keep untouched the prestige of authority ; I shall establish liberty without disorder, and power without violence. To justify my undertaking and my personal intervention in so serious a struggle, with some I will urge the value of my hereditary right; with others my principles ; and with all, the common interests of Protestantism, and the necessity of opposing the aggrandisement of France ; but I will accept nothing unless by the free vote of the nation, for a man can never thrust his will or his person on a great people !

Such were the. ideas that guided William. All the actions of his life were the application of these principles.

On October 10th, 1688, the Prince of Orange published a manifesto which contained the enumeration of the principal abuses of James's government. Thence resulted an evident proof: that James II. had sold to a foreigner the honour and interest of the English, and that he wished to destroy the laws and the religion of the country.

The prince offered himself as called by a great many members of the clergy, of the nobility, and by the wish of the people. He set forth that the rights of his wife, as well as of himself, imposed on him the obligation to watch over the safety .of the constitution and of the religion. His sole intention was to repair the injuries they had sustained, and to put the nation in a position to do itself justice. For this purpose a free parliament was necessary, formed, not after the new charters which had deprived the towns and boroughs of their rights, but after the ancient statutes and usages; for he did not come as a conqueror, but with the sole object of seconding the national wishes.[1]

Rarely great enterprizes succeed at the first stroke; one would say that it was necessary for them to whet themselves first against obstacles of all sorts. William, having embarked his expeditionary army at Texel, the 30th October, was repulsed by a fearful storm, which dispersed his fleet, and deprived him of the principal resources on which he depended; but nothing could subdue his perseverance. He re-embarked the 12th November, and on the 15th he touched at Torbay the soil of England. His standard bore these words, welcome to every English heart : " I shall maintain the Protestant religion and the liberties of England."

He kept his word.

James, on learning the disembarkation of Wil-

[1] Boulay (de la Meurthe), *Histoire de Jacques II.*, p, 147.

liam, opened his eyes, revoked a portion of the unjust and arbitrary measures which he had put into execution, and disavowed his alliance with Louis XIV. ; but the day had arrived, when concessions are nothing more than a signal of distress, and when kings recognise their faults only to expiate them.

The Prince of Orange arrived in London without meeting any obstacle. The most distinguished families had terrible reckonings to make with James ; the nation had overpowering grievances to be redressed; and the army could not remain faithful to a government which had made common cause with the enemies of its country.

The rallying cry of the English people was: "A free parliament, uo popery, no slavery !"

James fled, then returned to London, and then fled again to avoid being conducted to the Castle of Ham,[1] where William and his council had resolved to confine the fallen sovereign. The Prince of Orange succeeded. Will he abuse his triumph and the first enthusiasm of the people for their deliverer? William is not come to take a crown

[1] A private house, situated near London, on the banks of the Thames.

by assault : he is come to consolidate the destinies of England. Besides, he has destroyed the principle, regarded as inviolable and sacred, of heritage; it is impossible for him to combat this, but by another principle, the sovereignty of the people. One cannot replace an acquired and acknowledged right except by opposing to it another right legally acquired and legally recognised. There were not wanting counsellors, however, who advised him to seize upon power by right of conquest, as William the Conqueror had done, forgetting, without doubt, that six hundred yea.rs of civilization had made power to reside in the national right rather than in the sword. Others, also, urged him to seize the crown, representing to him the dangers of anarchy, that accommodating phantom which always serves as an excuse for tyranu y.

William remained immoveable, he would not usurp.

The peers and bishops, who were present in the capital, had assembled themselves at Westminster, and had formed a kind of provisional government. They presented him with an address, to take for the present the reins of government ; but to accept at the hands of the aristocracy alone a power, even temporary, was not the object of William. He assembled as soon as possible all the members of the two last parliaments held under Charles II., because these parliaments alone were considered free, the Honse of Commons of James having been elected under the control of the law which violated the freedom of elections; to them he added the Lord Mayor, the aldermen, and **fifty** members of the municipality of London,[1] and after he had united them with the Upper House, he engaged them to take measures the most efficacious for convoking a free parliament, as his declaration set forth. After having deliberated, these two houses went to St. James's,[2] and entreated the Prince of Orange to accept the government until the meeting of a national assembly.

William, thus authorised by all those who could at the moment represent the nation in the most legitimate manner, took on himself provisionally the administration, both civil and military, of the

---

[1] Hume, vol. i., p. 370.
[2] The Prince of Orange remained at the Palace of St. James, until the day when the Convention came to offer him the crown in the banquet-room of Whitehall, which was then the royal residence.

kingdom, and sent everywhere circular letters that they should proceed with the elections in conformity with the ancient statutes and usages. The troops were sent away from all the places where the elections were to take place; the greatest order prevailed in them as well as the greatest freedom; and on the 2nd of February, the Parliament, which took the name of Convention, met to decide legally the destinies of England. In this assembly, all the fundamental questions were freely handled and lengthily discussed. They adopted as a fundamental principle, that there existed an original contract between the king and the people; that James II. had violated it, and that the throne was vacant, and that William and Mary should be elected king and queen of Great Britain, but that to the prince alone should the administration be entrusted.

During these grave deliberations, which lasted nearly a month, the Prince of Orange had maintained a complete neutrality. Considering his only duty to be the maintaining of order, he had even repressed a petition carried in tumult to the Parliament, although it was in his own favour,' Full of

[1] Hume, vol. x., p. 381.

reserve and dignity, he remained impassible in the midst of the agitation of passions, and entered into no intrigue with the electors, nor with the members of parliament; they reproached him even for the dry manner so little agreeable towards those from whom he might hope for support; but the great mind of William disdained a popularity which could only be acquired by base actions.

He broke silence only towards the end of the deliberations, and announced that, if the power was noi yielded to him in a manner to satisfy his views and conscience, he would return to Holland, and leave the Convention to arrange its affairs itself, preferring, said he, a private life to a position which would give him immense difficulties, whilst taking from him the means of benefitting the country :-the lofty declaration of a man of spirit, who did not wish to reign from love of supreme rank, but to accomplish a mission, and secure the triumph of a cause.

The Convention did not consider it to be its duty to limit its work to the election of a new king : it attached to the act of recognition of William, a declaration of the rights of the English nation, in which all the gueranteee which they had claimed in the latter times were sanctioned, the royal prerogative reduced within just limits and more precisely defined than ever.

The Prince of Orange acted towards Scotland as he had towards England. He convoked a Convention after the manner most favourable to freedom of voting. This Convention conceded him the crown, without forgetting to proclaim at the same time the rights of the people. With regard to Ireland, it was in revolt against England : he went himself to subdue it.

William is the legitimate sovereign of the country, since he has been elected by the free suffrages of an assembly, which has itself been freely elected to this end by the nation. How is he going to consolidate his throne, he who, independently of the difficulties which a new government always encounters, will be beseiged by innumerable dangers, inherent in the circumstances of the times!

Externally, he has a formidable enemy. who always menaces him. James II. has preserved Ireland, and he is sustained by the armies of the greatest sovereign of Europe, a king whose desires are almost always accomplished, because he has great men to execute them. On the Continent, the allies of William implore his succour against the invasions of Louis XIV.; in the interior, it is necessary for him to attach to himself all parties, to appease all hatreds, to heal all wounds, by making two chambers, composed of so many diverse elements, concur in his views.

It is no longer with an unlimited sway like that of Elizabeth, but with liberty, that he must organise a country in fermentation, and repel an enemy who has only to say-I *wilt,* to be obeyed. He finds nothing a.round him but the elements of trouble and division.

The republicans see with vexation his installation, and the partisans of James a.re ready to convert in the eyes of the people all his misfortunes into faults, all his faults into crimes. The religious sects, which are all political, forsake him reciprocally, and if he protects one he displeases all the rest.

The Upper House is divided into two camps, each of which solicits power, and the party which does not govern, takes vengeance for its failure, by a resistance almost factious.

The House of Commons, although composed in a great measure of men favourable to the revolution, is full of defiance· against the royal authority, and full of the spirit of revenge against its own enemies; it is necessary that William should reassure it, and that he should at the same time restrain its reactionary passions.

What means, then, will he employ to surmount all these difficulties? One alone! and it will succeed. It is to remain faithful to the cause of the revolution which has called him, and to make it triumph, in the interior by his justice, externally by his courage.

Let us admire, in William, his cleverness in uniting the independence and firmness of a chief with the flexibility of a constitutional king.

He yields all that can be yielded without dishonour, and he holds firm by all that he believes to he conducive to the welfare of the country which had confided to him *its* destinies.

If the Parliament wishes to inquire into the causes which make important enterprises miscarry, if it wishes to acquire more independence, if it wishes to have submitted to it the treaties or diplomatic negociations, if it accuses ministers, if it finds fault with nominations,[1] if it disputes with

---

[1] The Parliament complained that the king had not nominated to the office of Justice of Peace, men of sufficiently

the king the disposition of the confiscated wealth in Ireland,[1] if it wishes even, through jealousy of military power, that William shall separate himself from his old battalions who have assisted him in all his battles,[2] the king yields; but on his side, the political chief is immoveable, when it is a question of the national honour, or of some great measure of justice. With respect to foreign concerns, one likes to see his perseverance in sustaining, notwithstanding numberless reverses and a factious opposition, a furious struggle against the enemies of his country, until he has obtained an advantageous peace.

As regards his domestic policy, one likes to see his constancy and his firmness when, having proposed a bill of general amnesty, which is rejected by the Parliament, he signs an act of grace which ought to have the same conciliatory effect; when, with the object of uniting parties, he causes a bill to be adopted which abolishes the penalties imposed by previous laws against the Nonconformists; when, with the same view, he presses the Parliament, repeatedly, to unite in a single

[1] Hume and Smollet, vol. xi., p. 397.
[2] *Idem,* vol. xi., p. 381.

church the Presbyterians and the Anglicans,[1] which would have blended in the same religious dogmas a great majority of the nation ; when, in fact, he opposes himself incessantly to the rigorous measures that were proposed to him against the Catholics,[2] and he forgets offences and pardons injuries.

Receiving all his strength from the national glory, William was always sufficiently strong to be just.

Whilst James II. had only irritated the nation by his declaration in favour of liberty of conscience, because under shelter of that liberty, it was thought that he would protect Catholicism; William, on the contrary, strengthened his power by toleration. The people suspected no mental reservation in a sovereign who had the same interests as themselves.

From the first moment of his reign, the king

[1] The Commons, guided by a spirit 'of intolerance, rejected this last measure, which was, however, in the interests nf the revolution.

[2] When the deputation from the Scottish Convention brought to William its declaration, it stated, among other things, that it hoped he would destroy heresy, he interrupted it for the purpose of declaring that it was not his intention to persecute.

showed his solicitude for the welfare of the people, by abolishing the tax on fire, which was very vexatious to the poorer classes. He evinced great impartiality in the nomination of new judges, letting his choice fall on the most estimable and the most independent men.

Notwithstanding there were then, as after all great political changes, frustrated ambitions, wounded interests, which had recourse to conspiracies in order to attempt the overthrow of the new government. But, let us observe, it was never the men of the revolution who employed these violent measures.

Although there was then an opinion opposed to the new government, which they called republican or revolutionary,[1] this party remained tranquil; which proves that, if it did not consider the cause of William as its own, it found, nevertheless, that he guaranteed the common interests against the selfsame enemies.

When a political action was brought, the accused was never withdrawn from his natural judges : sometimes the Parliament carried bills of attainder; but it was not then the Upper House that descended

[1] Hume and Smollet, vol. xi., p. 185.

to play the pitiful rôle of an e-:uepiroml tribunal; it •~ the representarion of the whole nation, which by its sentence wished to show its atu.dunent to the ~oT"emment. and its hatred of everything which menaced its existence.

There were also fanatical men, sneh as put the destinies of their country at the end of a poniard, who attempted the life of the king; but they were dismissed with eontempt to the ordinary tribunals, under the idea that, to give too much importance to such outrages would only enco~cre others.

The conspiracy which was made in 1696 against the life of William, only served to call forth an expression of general attachment to his pel'80n. The two Houses of Parliament again declared that he alone possessed legitimate rights, and they drew up an act of association, by which they engaged themselves to defend against all others the governments and the person of the king. This declaration, signed by an infinite number of the citizens of all classes, was a second popular sanction of the rule of William. Although the Parliament suffered itself occasionally to be drawn away from sound political views by reactionary passions and by pitiful susceptibilities, it must be confessed, nevertheless, that it often showed itself worthy of the great interests it had to maintain : in the first place, it discussed with conscientiousness and dignity the rights of the vanquished, as well as those of the conqueror, and openly established the basis on which the new government should rest. It procured the necessary guarantees against the encroachments of the crown. It hastened, above all, to repel all partnership with the tyrannical acts of the preceding reigns, and not only did it annul the decrees against Lord Bussell, Algernon Sidney, and other victims of the despotism of Charles II., but it even named a committee of inquiry directed against the authors of, and accomplices in, the sentence which had condemned them to death.'

The Houses desired, at first, to hold the king dependant on themselves, by voting the civil list only from year to year. It was not until 1697, when William had secured an advantageous peace to England, that they fixed a civil list for the whole duration of his reign. Thus, then, nothing had been precipitated, and the Parliament did not testify its confidence, until it had for nine years proved and experienced the royal authority.

¹ Hume, vol. x., p. 77.

Important ameliorations were then adopted by the Houses : among other innovations, they appropriated to each of the services an annual revenue.

They resolved that all persons should be taxed according to the just value of his· real and personal estate, whether the capital were landed or commercial property, or whether it was derived from employments, pensions, or professions.

They increased the guarantees of individual liberty, extending by a new bill the benefits of the *habeas corpus* to crimes of high treason, and confiscation no longer made part of the punishments pronounced against political offences. The triennial bill, which limited the duration of the parliaments to three years, was adopted.

They decided that the resolutions taken in the privy council should be signed by all those who should have advised or approved them; that whosoever held a pension or a lucrative place from the crown, could not be a member of the House of Commons; that the judges should receive a. fixed salary, and that they could not again be legally removed except by addresses from the two Houses; that no pardon sealed with the great seal of

England could prevail against an accusation instituted in Parliament by the House of Commons.[1]

Thus, whilst the king re-established order, and gave a new lustre to the English name, the parliament, on its side, secured public liberty. If, on home questions, the policy of William was grand and national, it was still more so with respect to foreign relations.

Since the day when their country being in the greatest danger, the people of Holland had intrusted him with power, William followed, whether as Prince of Holland, or as King of England, the same line of conduct.

The power of Louis XIV. had excited for a long time tht' jealousy of the sovereigns of Europe. They had all leagued themselves against the great king : but, abandoned by England, in 1678, Holland, Spain, and the Emperor of Germany had seen themselves compelled to acknowledge, by the peace of Nimegue, almost all the conquests of France. This peace had been i~ a great measure the work of Charles Il.'s treachery, for he had, through cowardice, sold to Louis XIV. the honour of his country, the interest of his allies, and had thus

[1] Hume and Smollet, vol. xi., p. 428.

allowed the opportunity to pass away of securing the preponderance of England. This treaty remained, then, for Great Britain, if not a monument of its shame, at least a proof of the dependanee and weakness of its government.

But William had not accepted the crown to continue the policy of the Stuarts. Scarcely had be arrived in London, when, far from seeking any foreign recognition, he, within twenty-four hours; sent back again to Versailles Barillon, the ambassador of Louis XIV., who was the able servant of his master, but the fatal counsellor of the Stuarts.

As soon as he finds himself at the head of the English people, he demands from the parliament subsidies for equipping his fleets, and for augmenting his armies.

He reconquered Ireland by the battle of the Boyne ; by the naval battle of the Hague, 1692, he destroys all the hopes of James, and repairs the disasters which his fleets have experienced at sea.

But, on the Continent, the arms of Louis XIV. are always victorious : at Fleurus, at Steinkerque, at Neurwinde, at Marseilles in Piedmont, as in the

Low Countries, on the Rhine as on the Ter,[1] William and his allies are beaten, and the enterprises of the English fleets against Dunkirk, Saint Malo, and the coasts of Brittany have all miscarried.

Nevertheless, the fertile genius of William derives more advantage from his defeats than his enemies from their successes. Louis XIV., who had formerly conquered the half of Holland and Flanders, all Franche-Oomte without a blow, cannot even march into the United Provinces, after the greatest efforts and the most sanguinary victories.

William remains the soul of the coalition, and encourages Spain, Holland, and Germany to maintain the struggle.

He goes every year from England to the Continent, to determine the plans of the campaign, and to put himself at the head of the armies ; every year he returns to England, to appease the fears of the Parliament, to gain its approbation, to explain to it his great designs, and obtain from it the necessary subsidies for continuing the war. Sometimes the Houses receive him with murmurs, but the people always follow him with acclamations.

[1] Marshal de Noailles gained a battle in Catalonia, on the banks of the Ter.

On opening the session of 1696, he declares that, notwithstanding the proposals for peace, IT IS WITH WEAPONS IN HAND THAT THEY MUST TREAT WITH FRANCE, and the Parliament replies, that, notwith> standing the sacrifices which the nation has made in men and in money, it will support him against' all enemies abroad, as well as at home.

At length, in 1697, his perseverance has triumphed over the fortune of Louis XIV., and success has crowned his efforts.

The peace of Ryswick is signed between France, England, Holland, and the Emperor of Germany. By this treaty, which was in every respect favourable to the honour and the commercial interests of England and the Low Countries, Louis XIV. recognized William III., and abandoned the cause of the Stuarts ; he restored to the allies of William a great portion of the towns which he had taken from them, and Lorraine to the son of Charles V.

Thus, then, William, in nine years, has snrmounted all the obstacles, interior and exterior, that opposed his designs; he has caused all the attempts of James II. to miscarry ; he has united in his favour almost the whole nation, and he has even managed to restore to England all her influence in the congress of kings.

The 3rd December, 1697, the king goes down to the Parliament and announces that he has attained his object in having concluded an honourable peace.

The chief of proud Albion is no longer, as was Charles II., the vassal of France ; he is become one of the arbiters of the fate of Europe, and in the south as well a.- in the north, in the east as in the west, they will do nothing without consulting him.

By his mediation [1] an end was put to the war iu Hungary, which had lasted fifteen years bet.ween Turkey and the Emperor of Germany ; and by the aid th~t he sends to Charles XII., he compels Poland and Denmark to conclude a peace with Sweden.

Even Louis XIV. disposes by anticipation, in conjunction with William, of the inheritance of Charles II. of Spain, whose death appeared to be approaching.

Several treaties of contingent division are agreed on between them; but it was difficult for two such vrond characters to be long united in their designs.

The will of the King of Spain, which declares

[1] Hume and Smollet, vol. xi., p. 379.

the Duke of Anjou sole inheritor of that monarchy, reanimates all the jealousies against France ; England. by its adherence or its resistance is about to decide the fate of Europe. Louis XIV., not being able to gain over the king as he had gained the Stuarts, endeavours by bribes to corrupt the influential members of parliament,[1] and William is compelled, by the attitude of the Houses, to aeknowledge for a time the accession of a Bourbon to the throne of Spain.

But the hostile attitude of the Parliament does not frighten William; he relies upon the people, and knows that by awakening the national feeling he will break down the obstacles that would prevent his sustaining his allies and the great interests of his country on the Continent. Public opinion is not slow in pronouncing itself. We will not, said the English, in the famous petition of Kent, be the slaves of parliaments any more than of kings. William dissolves the Houses, and in convoking new ones, the 13th of December, 1701, he opens the session by a speech wherein he developes all the depth and all the nationality of his policy. He asks them to support him in his views, to

[1] Hume and Smollet, vol. xi., p. 422.

secure public credit, to consider carefully the condition of the poor, to encourage commerce, and to improve the general tone of morality. He conjures them above all not to give advantage to the cause of their common enemy by abandoning the results of all their efforts on the Continent ; he urges them to seize the opportunity of securing the preponderance of England, by putting themselves at the head of Protestantism in Europe. And, finally, he appeals to all the sentiments of national honour.

This appeal was not made in vain. The House of Commons unanimously votes subsidies ; the House of Lords shows the same enthusiasm, and the speech of William is bought by the people and framed in the cottages,[1] as the most faithful representation of the conquests and of the policy of the revolution. It was the political testament of William, who died a few months after (8th March, 1702), but who might quit life with that inward satisfaction which a great man experiences who has secured the prosperity, the liberty, and the grandeur of his country.

[1] Hume and Smollet, vol. xii., p. 37.

CHAPTER III.

POLICY OF THE STUARTS.

FIRST PART. CHARLES I.

We have recalled the principal features of the life of William ; it is sufficient to show how much they differ from the acts which are now passing before our eyes in France.

The policy of 1830 is not the policy of 1688 ; it is quite the opposite.

It is not the system of William III., but the system of the Stuarts, which has been taken as a model.

To prove this, we are about to analyse the causes of the events which convulsed England during sixty-three years. In retracing this period, so full of interest, of the history of Great Britain, we shall see how much the unhealthy state of society, from 1640 to 1660, is analagous with our own in its struggles and in its passions, and we shall be led to the sorrowful conclusion that the eleven years which have just passed by in France, since 1830, resemble the epochs which commence revolutions, instead of resembling those which conclude them.

As it is not a dramatic comparison which we seek, but, on the contrary, a philosophic comparison, we believe it is rational to compare with each other those epochs which approach each other in the ideas which dominated society, in the spirit which guided power, although the principal events are not the same.

Of what importance is it if the frames are different. when the pictures which we are comparing have the same colours and represent the same subjects?

England had already suffered, in 1625, two great revolutions. The first arose in the thirteenth century, the era of the declaration of the Great Charter; the second took place in the sixteenth century, in consequence of the weakening of the nobility and of feudalism under Henry VII.,[1] and by the

[1] Henry VII. abolished, among other things, the feudal

religious reform violently executed by Henry VIII.

The first revolution had established rights ; the second had realized the benefices by disseminating through the country the wealth of the nobles and of the clergy.[1]

Now, as all great interests require ideas, colours, and ensigns for their representation, Protestantism in England became the emblem of all these national conquests.

Elizabeth had done more than confirm the interests of these revolutions, she had saved them. Thus her despotism had been more popular than liberty.

James I., the head of the unfortunate dynasty of the Stuarts in England, thought that he could preserve the absolute power of Elizabeth without having her genius, and enjoy the same authority in a different spirit, and with a contrary object. He

laws, "which threw obstacles in the way of the subdivision of fiefs."-Guizot, *Histoire de Charles I.*, vol. i., p. 2.

[1] In the division of lands made by William the Conqueror, the clergy received for their share 2801.5 manors, that is to say, more than a third of the wealth the kingdom.

The nobles alienated the greatest part of the vast dominions which Henry VIII. divided amongst them.

only sapped the foundations of the throne, and prepared the revolution which burst out in the reign of his son.

The government of James I. inspiring only contempt, the royal prerogatives, which, under Elizabeth, were regarded as the rights of the crown, were no longer considered to be other than abuses.

Frequently the people give a switch with which you may guide but never strike them.

As to the aristocracy, it had bowed before the throne ever since the accession of the Tudors, but with this reservation, to raise themselves always together with the liberties of the people.

When Charles I. ascended the throne, he found himself at the head of a power almost absolute over a people which already poasesaed all the legal means by which to shackle absolutism. The parliaments[1] had never ceased to assemble. Trial by jury existed. The towns had preserved their charters, the corporations their franchises, and men's minds were trained to political discussions

[1] Under Edward III. it had been ordered, that the Houses of Parliament should meet once in each year, and even oftener, if it were necessary.

by their habits of controversy on matters of religion.

The English knew then all the sources of liberty, if they were still unable to see how to turn them to account ; and now that power did not lead them according to the national interpretation of leading, they were about to claim free and perfect authority over the benefits beque~thed to them by their fathers; for there is no enjoyment where there exists the fear of losing.

The confidence of the people had passed from the crown to the parliament, because that a.lone appeared to guarantee the freedom which they had acquired, and the fulfilment of the prayer which they daily addressed to heaven.

The evils of society were patent, and yet there existed in the nation only a vague and indefinite desire for a better state of things.

Years glide away before a people puts its hand on the parts where its wounds lie. The more easy it appears to proclaim its actual griefs, so much the more do men's minds launch themselves into the mysticism of theories.

At length, Great Britain had arrived, in 1625, at one of those solemn periods, when a sovereign remains at the head of a labouring society only on the condition that he will direct it; and when he directs it only on the condition that he will favour and regulate the new ideas.

Nevertheless, the reign of Charles I. announced itself under happy auspices. " England promised itself happiness and freedom under a king whom at length it could respect."!

This hope was soon dissipated. From the very first, complaints manifested themselves. They reproached the government for protecting the Catholic religion, which, in England, had descended to the state of a political party ; they found fault with its negociations, its alliances, its carelessness regarding commerce, its employment of subsidies. Instead of condemning these perhaps too hasty complaints, by repressing the abuses which they exposed, the Government condemned their authors ; then distrust augmented, the parliament became more imperious, the king more irritated.

Desiring to turn aside public attention from

[1] Guizot, *Histoire de Charles I.,* vol. i., p. 3. We thought that we could not better describe the state of England under Charles I. than by citing several passages from the brilliant history of M. Guizot.

home affairs, by an expedition made in favour of Protestantism, Charles I. caused a. fleet to be equipped to succour the besieged in Rochelle.

But there are governments struck by death from their birth, the most national measures of which inspire only mistrust and discontent.

Charles I. demanded twenty vessels from the City of London towards the equipment of his fleet, and they answered him, that Elizabeth [1] had exacted less from them to repel the grand Armada of Philip II. The king determined that they should give them to him, and, notwithstanding these powerful resources, he failed twice before the energy of Richelieu.

The Parliament declared itself still more hostile, and its popularity increased in proportion to its hostility. Charles, after having dissolved it several times, recalled it, and recalled it to decide in its favour.

In 1628, the famous bill, known under the name of the Bill of Rights, was sanctioned by the King and the two Houses. This was not an extraordinary innovation : this bill made sacred acknow-

[1] Guizot, *Histoire de Charles t,* p. 32.

)edged liberties, or repressed abuses universally reprobated.

The king and the nation must have been great strangers to each other, before the one could regard as a grievous defeat and the other as a signal victory that which was only the confirmation of ancient rights.

Feeble and shortsighted powers think they have done all when, after having long struggled against public opinion, they are obliged to yield.

They have, however, shown nothing but their evil desires, intentions, and their weakness.

Charles believed that he was at the end of his trials, they were only just commencing; the Commons let their hatred burst out against the Duke of Buckingham, his counsellor, and threatened to impeach him. The king thought he had shown sufficient deference to the wishes of parliament, and that the time for concessions was passed. He thought to save his minister by keeping him near himself. The Duke of Buckingham was assassinated, and the nation dared to leap for joy. Irritated by so many outrages, Charles dissolved parliament, and resolved to govern alone; for eleven years England seemed quiet, but the agitation had only diffused itself over the whole surface of the body of society.

" For some time it was easy to govern. The citizens occupied themselves only with their private interests. No great debate, no lively emotion agitated the gentlemen in county meetings, the tradespeople in municipal assemblies, the sailors in the ports, the apprentices in the workshops. It was not that the nation languished in apathy, its activity had taken another course; it might have been supposed that it had forgotten in labour the overthrow of liberty. More haughty than fierce, the despotism of Charles troubled itself but little in this new state of things. This prince was not forming any vast designs, had no need of a glory strong and full of risk ; it sufficed him to enjoy with majesty his power and his rank. Peace did not require him to exact from the people any heavy sacrifices, and the people gave themselves up to agriculture, to commerce, to study, without any ambitious and agitating tyranny coming every day to harass their efforts and compromise their interests; public prosperity also developed itself rapidly, order reigned in the ranks of the citizens, and this flourishing and regular state gave to power the appearance of wisdom, to the country that of resignation." [1]

However, whilst he smothered complaints, the evils were not cured ; and the course of the government, although freed from the impediments of parliamentary discussion, became shortly neither more easy nor more clear on that account.

" Notwithstanding the energy and the zeal of his principal counsellors, notwithstanding the tranquillity of the country, notwithstanding the dignity of the king's manners, the government was without strength, and was held in no respect. Assailed by internal dissensions, ruled in turns by contrary influences, sometimes arrogantly shaking off the yoke of the laws, sometimes yielding before the most frivolous impediments, no system was for long persisted in by the king, indeed, he forgot every moment his own intentions."[2]

Charles hastened, as soon as he saw himself free from the control of the Houses of Parliament, to conclude a peace with France (1629) and Spain (1630), and thus to abandon the Protestant cause in Europe.[3]

[1] Guizot, vol. i., p. 64.   [2] Guizot, vol. i., p. 75.   [3] Ibid.

The influence of England had only decreased, and the standard of Britain was astonished at no longer inspiring respect, as in the time of Elizabeth.

" Pirates from Barbary came into the English Channel, and even into St. George's Channel, infesting the coasts of Great Britain. Such great incapability, and the danger resulting from it, did not escape the notice of experienced men. The foreign ministers who resided in London, informed their masters of this state of things ; and shortly, notwithstanding the known prosperity of England, the opinion spread itself all over Europe, that the government of Charles was weak, imprudent, and ill secured. At Paris, Madrid, and the Hague, his ambassadors were several times treated slightingly and with disdain." [1]

"To frivolous and unskilful tyranny, a daily increase of tyranny becomes necessary; that of Charles was, if not the most cruel, at least the most unjust and most abusive that England had ever suffered. Without being able to allege as an excuse any political necessity, without dazzling men's minds by any great result, in order to satisfy obscure wants and

[1] Guizot, vol. i., p. 78.

accomplish desires without aim, it set aside and offended old established rights, as well as more recent wishes, ignoring the laws and the opinions of the country, and the avowals and promises of the king himself, making a random trial, according to circumstances, of every species of oppression, adopting in short the rashest resolutions, the most illegal measures, not for the sake of securing the triumph of a system consistent and formidable in itself, but to support by daily expedients a power that was always embarrassed. Subtle counsellors, incessantly ransacking the old registers to discover therein some precedent for further iniquity, laboriously exhumed the abuses of the past, and raised them up as rights of the throne. Did they sometimes doubt the compliance of the judges, or did they wish to direct their influence! The Star Chamber, the North Court, and a crowd of other jurisdictions not controlled by the common law, were charged to take their places." [1]

In 1636, the Star Chamber was ordered to punish for the publishing of Puritan pamphlets.

"The iniquity of the proceeding equalled the cruelty of the sentence."[2]

[1] Guizot, vol. i., p. 80.   [2] Guizot, vol. i., p. 112.

" Did discontent appear too general in any county, its militia was disarmed, and troops were sent thither whom the inhabitants were required to lodge and feed."[1]

In the towns the chief citizens, in the country a considerable number of the small gentry, and almost all the freeholders, carried further than others, in matters of religion particularly, their rage and their opinions.

"Amongst them a passionate attachment to the Reformation prevailed, an ardent desire to adopt the results of its principles, a profound hatred of all that preserved any resemblance to Popery, or that reminded them of it ; for the reformed religion proclaimed the freedom of civil society, and abolished the usurpations of spiritual power in temporal matters.[1]

" On political subjects, the effervescence, although less general and less disorderly, did not fail to spread itself.

" In the bosom of the lower classes, whether it was the result of easy circumstances to which they had before been strangers, or whether it was the consequence of religious belief, ideas about and

[1] Guizot, vol. i., p. 94.   [1] Guizot, vol. i, p. 103.

desires for equality, until then unknown, began to circulate. In a more elevated sphere, some rude and proud spirits, detesting the court, despising the impotency of the ancient laws, and giving themselves up with passion to the freedom of their own thoughts, dreamed, in the solitude of their studies, or in private conversations, about institutions more simple and more efficacious. Others, agitated by aims less pure, strangers to all faith, cynics in their manners, and thrown by their humour, or by chance, into the ranks of the malcontents, were hoping for a revolution which should give scope to their ambition, or free them at least from all curb.

" Fanaticism and licence, sincerity and hypocrisy, both respect and disdain for the old institutions, lawful wants and ill-regulated desires, all concurred to foment the national anger ; all rallied against an authority, the tyranny of which warmed with the same hatred men of the most dissimilar natures, whilst its imprudence and its weakness gave to the smallest factions, and to dreams the most audacious, activity and hope."!

" The government, notwithstanding its embar-

1 Guizot, vol. i., p. 110.

rassment, was confident and proud. To justify itll conduct, it spoke often, and with emphasis, of the evil spirit which was propagating itself; but its momentary fear awoke not its prudence, and whilst fearing, it disdained its enemies. Even the neceseity it was under of making tyranny more intolerable each day, did not enlighten it, and it applauded itself all the more for its power, because increasing dangers obliged it to use still greater rigour." [1]

Charles I. had entered, without wishing it, on the gloomy path, where it is no longer a question of governing, but of sustaining himself, where justice is no longer thought of but severity. The men of the people had been the first victims of the persecutions.

" The only martyrs as yet belonged to the people, none of them were distinguished by their names, their talents or their fortunes ; many of them even were but little considered in their professions, before their accusation, and the opinions they had maintained were in many respects only those of the fanatical sects especially trusted by the multitude. Proud of their courage, it soon accused the upper classes of weakness and apathy.

[1] Guizot, vol, i., p. 110.

'Now,' said they, 'the honour which usually dwells in the head has, like the gout, descended to the feet."[1]

But soon the upper classes of society experienced the same affronts, and suffered the same persecutions ; public opinion aroused itself, and compelled the king to convoke, in 1640, a new parliament, destined not to be dissolved before it had overthrown him.

However, when this assembly, which afterwards received the name of the Long Parliament, had actually met, the nation was still uncertain.

" Whatever might be its displeasure, to any violent design it was a stranger. Sectarians, in certain places the multitude, and some men already compromised as chiefs of the growing parties, were the only persons who nourished darker passions, or had more decided views. The public had approved and supported them in their resistance, but without associating itself with any other schemes, indeed without suspecting that such existed. Long reverses had placed many good citizens in doubt, if not as to the legality, at least as regarded any profit to be derived from the ardour and obstinacy

[1] Guizot, vol. i., p. 116.

of the last parliaments. They recalled without blame, but with regret, the rudeness of their language, and the disorder of the scenes which had agitated them ; they promised on their own part more prudence : under the influence of this disposition, the elections returned a House of Commons opposed to the Court, decided on redressing wrongs, and in which all the men whom their opposition had rendered popular, took their seats, yet composed for the greater part of peaceable citizens, free from all engagement to party, mistrustful of passions, of secret combinations, of hasty resolutions, and flattering themselves that they could reform abuses without alienating the king, without hazarding the repose of the country.

" In this state of mind, the moral situation of the Parliament was false; because it was by it, and for its profit that the revolution was accomplished ; constrained to effect it, and at the same time to disown it, its actions and language contradicted themselves by turns, and it fluctuated painfully between audacity and cunning. violence and hypocrisy.

" Each day it was compelled to proceed by opposite paths, to make contrary efforts. W'hat it begged from the Church, it repelled in the State ; it followed necessarily that, changing so incessantly its position and language, it invoked by turns the principles and passions of democracy against the bishops; the royalist or aristocratic maxims and influences against the rising republicans. It was a strange spectacle to see the same men demolish with one hand, and support with the other ; sometimes preaching innovation, sometimes anathematizing the innovators ; alternately rash and timid, rebels and despots at the same time ; persecuting episcopacy in the name of the rights of liberty, the Independents in the. name of the rights of power; arrogating to themselves, in abort, the privileges of insurrection and of tyranny, whilst declaiming each day against tyranny and insurrection."

This state of uncertainty and of contradiction could not last. Since the opening of Parliament, Charles had been obliged to yield to the torrent of opinion. But his concessions had been to him as disastrous as his resistance. Desirous of regaining some popularity, without however satisfying the just demands of the people, he desired to flatter them through their hatreds by persecuting the papists, *l'ictim,* devoted to the reconciliation of the prince with the country.

But injustice has never strengthened a throne. The king had opened the gate to the passions of hatred, without knowing where they would stop, without foreseeing whom they would first strike. The vengeance of Parliament fell heavtly on the unfortunate Lord Strafford, on the only man perhaps who, at the commencement of the reign, could have saved the monarchy, and who now was about to become the victim of those measures which he had carried out contrary to his own convictions, out of attachment to his sovereign. Charles abandoned his minister to his executioners ; but with the head of Lord Strafford was about to fall also the last prestige of royalty. This forsaking of his friend, evidenced at the same time the weakness of the king and the cowardice of the man.

Parties had tried all legal measures; all the resources of reason and of justice were exhausted: : passions alone remained. The struggle was about to begin. We know how it ended.

CHAPTER IV.

TH H P O L IO Y OF T HE ST U AR TS.

SECOND PART. CHARLF..8JI.

Oharles I. miserably expiated his own as well as his father's faults ; but how many reasons may be urged in extenuation of his errors! Educated in the principles of absolute authority, the example of the kings who had preceded him must have led his judgment astray, and made him mistake the just complaints of his people for factions declamations, and the convulsions of society ill at ease for vulgar seditions.

But, after him, it was madness for a man to deceive himself, for his example showed forth, in letters of blood, in England's history, where lay the harbour and where were the sunken rocks. However, thirty-nine years were destined to glide by, and five governments were successively to come and dash themselves in pieces against public opinion, before England should have cast the anchor of its liberties.

Our object is not to write the progress of events which followed the death of Charles I., we shall only say a word about the eleven years which preceded the restoration of his son.

The struggle, which overturned the throne of England, had not been, as was later the revolution of 1789, one of those violent commotions which are at the same time social, political, and intellectual; which attack all received opinions, all the upper classes, all existing interests, and which ehake the country to its foundations, because the people rise at once to free themselves from feudal oppressions, to attain the relief which had been refused to them, to possess themselves of rights which never had been theirs.

In England, civilization had effected by degrees in several centuries that which, in France, had been, so to speak, but the work of one day.[1]

That makes the immense difference between the two revolutions ; also, nothing in these two events, excepting the royal catastrophe, can be compared,

[1] See the reflections at the commencement of the preceding chapter.

neither the eausea that produced, nor the effects which resulted from them.

The English Revolution changed neither manners nor institutions, and left behind it nothing but an immense national claim, known under the name of the Act of Naviga.tion.₁ Cromwell, who, during five yea.rs, occupied the first place, because religious and political fanaticism demanded a chief, could not establish anything. He was only a clever steersman during the tempest. Raised to powP-r by storms, a calm had destroyed him. Instead of creating new interests, he had always to wrestle against those ancient habits of liberty which were deeply rooted in the nation.s Also, what a difference in the popularity enjoyed by the men of the two revolutions. The members of the convention which had voted the death of Louis XVI., were employed as ministers by a prince who returned with all Europe for his support, whilst Charles II., freely recalled by the people, not only put to death the regicides and exhumed the skeleton of Cromwell to hang it on a gibbet ; but, twenty-nine

---

[1] The famous Act of Navigation proposed by the Council of State to the Parliament of 1681.

[1] See Villemain, *Histoire de Cromwell,* p. 382.

years later, and after a new revolution had taken place, Ludlow,[1] who had returned to his country, could not remain, but was obliged to save himself by flight from the prosecution which Parliament had directed against him.

These reflections seemed needful for the purpose of explaining the enthusiasm with which the people returned of their own accord to royalty. The assembly which recalled Charles II. was the first free Parliament which had been convoked since 1649; and what is worthy of remark, is, that the Bill of Convocation emanated from the remains of the Long Parliament, and excluded from the political assemblage those who were openly known as Royalists, er who had taken up arms in favour of either Charles I. or his son.

That which took place in England, in 1660, may then be considered as a veritable revolution, which had the people for its support, the Parliament for its organ, and a general for its instrument. In fact, Monk, who had remained neutral

[1] Ludlow, who had voted for the death of Charles I., and who had been exiled under Charles IL, returned after the revolution of 1688, and requested to serve in the war with Ireland; William III. would have employed him; but the animosity of the people would not allow him to do so.

until the last moment,[1] would not have supported the return of the king if he had not thought that this reetoretion was in accordance with the then wishes of the greatest pa.rt of the nation.

Whatever material power a chief possesses, he cannot, to suit his own pleasure, dispose of the destinies of a great people; there is no real strength in any man's policy who doesn't make himself the instrument of the wishes of the majority. Henry VIII. ch~ged the religion of the country, because this change w88 already in the thoughts and in the interests of the majority ; without this he had not succeeded. The Stuarts miscarried in the same attempt from contrary causes.

The national movement then, in 1660, was all in favour of the recall of Charles II., and all concurred to win to him men's minds. This prince, at the age of sixteen, had fought for his father, and had endeavoured to save him at the head of a part of the English fleet which had revolted against the Parliament. Later, he came, sword in hand, to claim the crown, and only escaped with difficulty from the grasp of the conquering Orom-

[1] See in support of this assertion, *Hiataire de Cromwell*, by Villemain.

well, after the battle of Worcester. Recalled by the wish of the nation, he presented himself with these glorious antecedents and with the interest which misfortune overcome always inspires. His gracefulness of spirit, the affability of his manners prepossessed in his favour, and filled all hearts with joy and hope. But, during his exile, Charles II. had become a stranger to the manners, to the institutions, to the religion of his country ; misfortune, which tempers the soul or else blights it, had destroyed his energy ; he returned with interests opposed to those of the parties which had recalled him, and forgot that he found England tranquil only because it was weary, but that it was still divided by " the same questions about religious tolerance and political liberty which must be resolved since they cannot be suppressed." [1]

Four parties at that time represented, under a religious form, as many different shades of politics : the Independents or Republicans; the Presbyterians, who, with the other Protestant sects, formed the nonconformists; and lastly, the Anglican royalists and the Catholic royalists.

The Presbyterians had effected the revolution

[1] Villemain, *Histoire de Cromwell,* p, 446.

by allying themselves with the Independents. They made the counter-revolution by uniting themselves to the Anglicans; they formed then, together with the party to which they had joined themselves, the majority of the nation. '

Does it not seem that simple reason would tell the king that he should lean for support on that majority, which had recalled him, by favouring its desires and its religion? Should he not have sought to cement the union of the nonconformists and the Anglicans, and have profited by the suddenly awakened feeling of the nation, to assure th'.e liberties of England by giving it wise laws, and its foreign influence by honourable conduct?

But, by nature and by character, Charles II. was,sure to be opposed to such a policy.

By nature, that is ~o say as a Stuart, he could not rely on the Presbyterians, who were the authors of the revolution, nor on the Independents, who had given it so fatal an issue. The Anglicans and the Catholics seemed then to him to be the only natural supporters of his throne,¹ for, in

---

¹ He never was able to overcomehis repugnance to Monk and Admiral Montague, because of their republican antecedents; and even the Anglicans became soon the object of his nspicion.

politics as in physics, bodies neither draw towards nor separate from each other but by natural affinity or repulsion.

By character, Charles II. could not adopt a system of conciliation combined with greatneee. All the scenes which had troubled his life since his. infancy,. instead of producing in him deep convictions, had only created doubt in his heart. He despised both men and destiny ; men, because he eaw around him the champions of every govemment, adulators in succession of the republic of. Cromwell and of royalty; and he despised destiny, because he saw in the course of so many contradictory events; only the freaks of fortune. Penetrated by this political Atheism, he thought that a habit of skilful dissimulation would suffice to deceive mankind ; and trusted to chance to get through all dangers. He believed that by replacing ideas of honour and glory with the development of material interests, by destroying faith with craft, and eon-. sciences with corruption, he could get out of the labyrinths of political passions ; as regarded the nation, little did he care whether it lost itself therein.

The acclamations which had saluted the return

of the eon of Charles I. had not ceased resounding, before the king had already displeased all parties. Not daring to support the old royalists (called cavaliers) for fear of irritating the men of the revolution, not daring to trust himself to these last from natural antipathy, he was ungrateful [1] from cowardice and unjust from a feeling of distrust.

A people should never put confidence in a prince, who, in order to ascend a throne, is obliged to tranquillize men,s minds by a declaration, and to flatter parties by promising much; for the necessity of such manifestoes proves sufficiently, that he has not the same interests as the nation, and that hie person inspires doubts which even his words cannot calm.

The declaration of Breda bore on two little essential points : the disbanding of the army and a general amnesty.

The army was, in fact, disbanded, but only to be immediately reorganised. The amnesty was rendered null by the great exceptions ; Scotland and Ireland were not comprised therein.

[1] The royalists, obliged to capitulate in the town of Colchester, were sent by Cromwell to America, and sold as slaves. Charles II., restored to power, forgot to redeem them. (Chateaubriand, *Melangea Histo_riques*, p. 152.)

The fear of anarchy was eagerly taken advantage of by the government to excuse arbitrary measures. A commotion in London of some sectarians, was the signal for persecutions against the Noncom" formists and Presbyterians. A bill was drawn up for the security of the king and the government ; they did not confine themselves to punishing acts, they extended the penalties to simple projects, to writings, to opinions, even to simple words. Every *enterpri,e* against the person of the king was entitled a crime of high treason. This word *enterpriu,* says Boulay (de la Meurthe },[1] was assuredly very vague ; they might have replaced it with the term *attempt,* as we have seen in our days, without making the law more just, or the crime better defined. Charles II. had only one study, that of finding means to procure for himself sufficient money to meet his useless expenditure: he assembled his parliament, and spoke of the national glory with'. the sole object of making it grant him subsidies. After having abandoned Dunkirk to the French for five millions, he sold the interests and honour of his country to Louis XIV. for a weight

[1] Boulay (de la Meurtbe), *Histoire de Charles II.,* t. i., p. 60.

of gold. Such conduct was certain soon to lead the Parliament and the nation back again to hostile feelings, and all the more because the secret protection accorded to the Catholics helped to augment the general distrust.

To divert these sentiments, Charles resolved, 1664; to make war with Holland, a country that he detested, because of the republican forms of its government, and which he reproached with having given an asylum to his dissatisfied subjects, forgetting that when he was himself proscribed[1] he had found protection there.

This war, which was begun from caprice, was ended from very weariness, after some victories and some reverses; but the peace, concluded in 1667 by the treaty of Breda, was regarded by the English as dishonourable for them; and as if Providence would mark this reign with the seal of reprobation, the plague came at this time to desolate the kingdom, and a fire destroyed a great part of London.P

[1] Boulay (de la Meurthe), *Hiatoire de Charles II.*, t. i., p. 98.

[2] It is curious to remark, that all reigns which have been disastrous for their country have been signalized by some great disaster, such as pestilence, floods, fire, or famine.

Whilst in England the sovereign used all his skill to spread traps and snares for those parties. who desired an honourable policy ; in France, on the contrary, there was a young king who thought only of the glory of his country.

Louis XIV. claimed at that time all the Spanish Netherlands as the patrimony of his wife, the daughter of Philip IV., and had seized, on his way, Flanders and Franche-Comte. This unexpected invasion had alarmed Europe. Holland, although allied to France, saw with fear so formidable a neighbour. The Emperor of Germany prepared himself for war. Sweden dreaded the alliance of France and Denmark, and public opinion in England enthusiastically made common cause with the alarms of the Continent. The king, compelled to submit himself to these manifestations, charged Sir William Temple, a man whose patriotism equalled his capacity, to conclude the treaty of the TRIPLE ALLIANCE, which opposed to France the united forces of England, Sweden, and Holland. But Charles only yielded against the grain to this policy. He perceived every day more and more. that his cause was not that of the nation, and that he could not reign without relying on a foreign force which would give him the means of quelling his internal enemies, and of dispensing consequently with all national representation.

For the execution of a plan so dangerous, it was necessary that he should have recourse to all the means that stratagem can invent, that policy admits of, but which morality always reproves.

Governments which are not popular enough to govern by uniting their citizens, nor sufficiently Btrong to keep them bound in one general oppression, can only support themselves by feeding discord between parties.

Charles II., who had himself at first persecuted the nonconformists, gave them up afterwards to the persecutions of the An~licans, to the end, said he, that they might better understand the repose which they would enjoy, if the Catholics had the upper hand.'

He congratulated himself upon his first successes in this tortuous path, saying to Lord Essex : " I have so well lighted the wa.r between the Anglican clergy and the Nonconformists, that they will not bethink themselves hereafter of uniting to combat my designs." [9]

[1] Mazure, t. i., p. 88.
[3] Boulay (de la Meurthe), t. i., p. 133.

But wickedness, however skilful it may be, is wrong to boast of its passing victories; for, at the last, it is justice alone that triumphs. The hopes of Charles were not realized in the sequel. The fear of the dangers which menaced them equally, the general antipathy to the Catholics, compelled the nonconformists to reunite themselves with the Anglicans, for the purpose of resisting the encroachments of power, and from that time embarrassments increased, and the opposition became menacing.

In the Parliament of 1670, Lord Lucas delivered this accusation: " Men hoped everything," he exclaimed, " from the re-establishment of the king; the subjects were to be comforted, the nation was to be happy and flourishing, and, instead of this, never have the burdens been so weighty : and real strength and the glory of England are diminishing day by day."[1]

Charles II. had signed the treaty of the triple alliance with the firm intention not to remain faithful to it, and basely to abandon his allies. The Emperor of Germany had offered to enter with him into this alliance against France, and he had

[1] Boulay (de la Menrthe), t. i., p. 136.

refused. The Duke of Lorraine had made him the same proposal, and when the latter, attacked and despoiled by France!¹ because of this offer, asked his assistance, he coldly said that *it was a misfortune Ickick he must endure.*

The king has already divided his enemies by exciting them against each other; now, the finishing stroke of his culpable skill will be to conclude shameful treaties through popular men, and to fight against Protestantism with men who were themselves Protestants. With this object he will always have a double policy and a double counsel. He will secretly combat the measures taken ostensibly by his ministers, will make them endure all the responsibility of embarrassments which he himself shall have caused, and, as regards foreign policy, will nullify all the negociations of his ambassadors, by ranging himself directly, through secret agents, on the side of the enemies of his country. By the deceitful cha.rm of his words, he will obtain the sanction of national men for his anti-national views, which will give him the double advantage of hiding the perfidy of his projects by the instrument

---

¹ Louis XIV. in fifteen days seized upon Lorraine.

L

of which he will make use, and of making unpopular the men who, in opposition, would be dangerous heads of party.

It is thus that Charles II. causes to be presented to Parliament, in 1670, by the keeper of the Great Sea.l, Bridgeman, a demand for subsidies, urging the necessity of arming against France and of sustaining the Protestant cause, whilst, without the knowledge of this minister, he at the same time is assuring Louis XIV. that his fleet shall not act except in conjunction with his own, and that he is increasing his land army solely for the purpose of fanning the evil passions of his country and of establishing Catholicism therein. In this way he destroys or renders unpopular all the men whom he employs ; with the same duplicity he is going to make use of Sir William Temple.

But he is a man who will not suffer himself to he trifled with by the king, and who will avenge himself by a brilliant popularity, and a vehement opposition, for any share he may have had in the support of a contemptible power. Ashley Cooper, Earl of Shaftesbury, was at the same time, under this reign, the author of the most unpopular measures, and the warmest instigator of the resistance of the Houses, and the friend of those laws which were most favourable to liberty.'

Meanwhile Louis XIV. having promised the king two hundred thousand pounds sterling a year, on condition that England should aid France in the conquest of the republic of the United Provinces, war, for the second time, was declared against Holland, in 1672.

Strong in this alliance, Charles revived the martial laws, which had been formally abolished by the petition of rights; he imposes severe penalties upon seditious speeches, and has recourse to a new perfidy by which he may mislead popular feeling.

The Nonconformists whom he has himself persecuted, and whom he afterwards caused to be persecuted by the Anglicans, he will now appear to ta.~e under his protection, and publishes an act of toleration which has for its only aim to favour Catholicism.

The Parliament, convoked in 1673, is irritated to the greatest degree by this measure, and represents to the king that he has not the right of sus-

₁ To him we are indebted for the law of Habeas Corpus, which passed in the session of 1679.

pending laws ; that the act of toleration cannot be promulgated without the consent of parliament. To give a wrong direction to these remonstrances, Shaftesbury uselessly expends all his eloquence to show how much to the interest of the nation is the war against Holland ; the Houses return to the exposition of their grievances, and moreover every English heart was already beating in favour of the young Prince of Orange, who had arrested Louis XIV. by opposing to his victorious arms the emperor, the empire, and Spain.

The position of the government was serious: men gave the king the most imprudent advice, and a *coup d/ltat* became imminent; but the character of Charles was adverse to such extreme measures, which compel tyranny to be open. He enters the House of Parliament, and assumes the appearance of yielding with a good grace, and destroys the edict which had raised so many recriminations. Shaftesbury, the responsible minister, the promoter of this unpopular act, feels that the whole blame is about to fall upon himself; suddenly he turns round against his colleagues, attacks with all the superiority of his talents and the power of his eloquence, a. financial plan of the Chancellor of the

Exchequer, which he gives to the vengeance of the public, and throws himself into opposition, saying that a king who abandons himself, deserves to be abandoned by others.

The ministry was dissolved, parliament was satisfied, and the national party believed that it had obtained an important victory ; nevertheless the ministers alone were changed, the policy was to remain the same. The country soon perceived this truth ; successive prorogations of the Houses showed that the Court dreaded the expression of discontent raised by the war on the Continent, which was becoming wearisome.

In the session of 1674, the grievances of the nation made themselves heard with power. The Commons declared, among other things, that the religion of the State was menaced by the marriage of the heir of the throne with a princess who did not profess the established religion ; they demanded who the perfidious councillors were who had broken the treaty of the triple alliance ? By whom had the last treaty with Louis XIV. been concluded! If it was to intimidate the Parliament that the army was encamped at the gates of London? In short, said they, these subsidies which we have lavished on you for the support of the power of England against the ambition of France, to what purpose have they been devoted! And why has war with the States-general been made without our knowledge?

These energetic complaints proved to the king that the moment was arrived for again ceding to public opinion; no one knew better than he how to dispel the storm by a simulated concurrence with the wish of the Houses. In the preceding year, he had torn the act of toleration without renouncing his projects in favour of Catholicism; now he is about to propose peace with the formal intention of being as useful to Louis XIV. by his neutrality as by his co-operation; in the same way as his apparent concession about religion, in 1673, has allowed him to continue an unpopular war, so the satisfaction he gives in 1674, in his foreign policy, will allow him to stifle complaints about internal grievances.

Peace was concluded with the States-general, and the Parliament separated happy in having compelled the Court to this peace; so easy is it for a sovereign to content a parliamentary opposition, and make it trust in his good faith, by deceitful promises.

During the four years which passed by, until the peace of Nimegue, political intrigues of all kinds afflicted England. On the one side, the king bought votes and consciences, and put off as long as he could the sessions of Parliament, to the end that he might not be forced to a more active policy against France ; on the other hand, Louis XIV. gave money to both the king and the opposition in the Houses, in order that intestine divisions might keep England dependant upon himself. The honour of the country also was for sale, and, in the midst of this universal corruption, the national interest was nothing more than a vessel struck by all winds, and which, without a rudder a.nd without a pilot, has hope only in the waves which may drive her into port.

In the meantime, the want of activity on the part of the government in the affairs of the Continent was exciting the suspicion of the people; the king offered to the belligerent parties his mediation for peace, with the secret design of making this mediation decidedly in favour of France. The better to mak~ them believe that his projects were decidedly national, Charles II. again ~ommissioned Sir William Temple to go to the Hague as ambassador extraordinary.

This minister, a truly good man, reflecting upon the ill success of the treaty of the triple alliance, wished, before accepting this new mission, to understand all the king's intentions, and to make him hear the truth. He blamed the steps taken by the Government, both at home and abroad; he declared to the king that he could not resist the wishes of the nation, and that his troops would not enable him to do so; finally, he cited to him the well known speech of a man for whom Charles had much esteem: " That a King of England would be the greatest of kings, if he would be the man of his people; but that he would be nothing, if he desired to be anything more." [1] The king, who knew better than any one how to cover his dissimulation by the outward appearance of frankness, and the most gracious *abandon,* shaking him by the hand, answered: " Go, depart ! I wish to be the man of my people.">

Temple, convinced, departed, and was basely deceived. Here is a good opportunity for remarking how much it is to be regretted that men who have at heart a great love of their country, a great desire to see it powerful and respected, should con-

[1] Hume, vol. x., p. 73.   [2] Mazure, t. i., p. 139.

sent to serve a government which makes them the instruments of its disgraceful projects. Proud of their capacities and of the purity of their intentions, they believe, when they take office, that they can direct politics in a better course; but their desire breaks against. a resistance stronger than itself. They do not save the power they serve, and in serving it they betray, against their wishes, the cause which they would make triumphant.

Negociations were opened and broken oft' many times until 1677, according to the different chances of the war; but when Louis XIV., who had struggled with success against nearly all Europe, had, in six weeks, taken the three greatest strongholds in the Netherlands, this new conquest alarmed England, and the Parliament insisted that they should make an alliance, offensive and defensive, with the States-general. At this period the Prince of Orange came to England to wrest Charles II. from the influence of France.

The king received him with eagerness, gave him his niece in maniage, and promised him that he would declare war with France, unless he obtained entire satisfaction for Holland. But at the same time he let Louis XIV. know, by his ambassador, that he would make all possible sacrifices to remain at peace with him: "For," said he, to Barillon, " I like better to depend upon the king, your master, than on my own people."?

Thns forewarned, Louis XIV. eludes a.ll the feigned menaces of the ambassadors, increases his pretensions, and follows up his conquests.

Notwithstanding, the King reassembles the Pat'- liament on the 15th of January, 1678, speaks of the danger in which Holland is, obtains a subsidy of two millions of pounds sterling, to arm eighty veesels, levies in six weeks twenty thousand men, and sends them into Flanders. Temple concerts with the united provinces rigorous measures against France. In six days, this skilful negociator concludes a treaty which obliges England to declare war, if Louis XIV. does not engage to abandon Flanders and Belgium in two months. They p~pare themselves, in England and Holland, for renewing the straggle. The nation believes that its honour is about to be avenged, and its interests worthily considered ; but soon they learn that all is changed, that, through the medium of a subaltern agent, Charles has come to an understanding

[1] Mazure, *Histoire de la Revolution de* 1688,t. i., p. 201.

with the powers, that Temple has been deceived, England betrayed, and that the courts of France, Sweden, a~d England, have unitedly agreed at Nimegue on the conditions of peace.

Six millions, in fact, had bought the neutrality of Charles, the promise of not reassembling the Parliament during six months, and of disbanding the army. The treaty of Nimegue (1678) preserved to France nearly all its conquests; it injured equally the interests of Holland, Spain, Germany, and England. Charles II·. might have been the arbitrator of Europe-he preferred being the tributary and the slave of Louis XIV.

The knowledge of this treaty deeply irritated the English nation. It said to itself: Here, then, is the result of all our sacrifices during eighteen yea.rs ! The immense sums which we have voted for the equipment of our fleets and for the maintenance of so great a land army, have been used only to dishonour us and effect the loss of our influence in Europe.

" Whilst Spain, Holland, the Empire, and the Princes of Germany," says Hume, "were calling upon England with a. loud voice, to lead them to victory, to liberty, and offered to make her more glorious than she had ever been before, her king, from base motives, had secretly sold her to Louis XIV., and allowed himself to be corrupted into betraying the interests of his people."[1]

This was the most glorious moment of the reign of Louis XIV., and the most humiliating of the reign of Charles II. ; for the King of France gave him nothing for England in exchange for his condescension; on the contrary, he put a duty on English merchandize, which at that time was an innovation,[1] he prohibited the trading of English vessels with the commerce of Genoa," which proves that cowardice is never profitable.

The peace of Nimegue put an end to the differences between Great Britain and the Continent ; but Charles had not seen the last of his trials ; he will be, until his death, the object of the contempt of Louis XIV., a prey to the factious hostility of the Parliament, and unceasingly menaced by conspiracies and insurrections of the people.

Nothing evidences more strongly the uneasiness of a society than when some unforeseen incident, trifling in itself, comes suddenly to rouse all spirits,

[1] Hume, vol. x., p. 61.
[2] Hume, vol. x., p. 397.   [1] Mazure, t. L, p. 371.

to raise every passion, and to lead to results which, in ordinary times, the greatest events only would be capable of producing.

The protection accorded to the Catholic party by the king, with such perseverance and dissimulation, had inspired the nation with so much fear and so much distrust, that it one day listened with marked favour and with surprising credulity to a vulgar man of impure morals, who came to unfold ~he improbable secrets of a Papist plot against the country and the State; and this vague declaration, which rested only on the word of a worthless man, brought to the scaffold Lord Stafford and other victims of this infernal machination.

Then, after this storm had passed, the conspiracies of the popular party commenced which sought its leaders amongst the early ministers of the king, it even treated with his own son; Lord Russell and Sidney, and many others were beheaded on account of their too hasty desire for liberty.

After this the king believed that the social dissolution had proceeded so far as would permit him to execute the project which he had been contemplating for twenty years. He dissolved the Parliament at Oxford, and reigned without control.

Were there no plain facts by which we could judge Charles II., we could form a just idea of his baleful influence, by copsidering how he employed the men who served him, and how he always sacrificed them to the passing interests of the moment ; Clarendon, to whom in a great measure he owed his crown, is abandoned by him to the censures of the Parliament, and exiled. Charles neglects the virtuous Ormond, abuses the devotion of Temple, and, towards the end of his reign, it is to Jeffries he gives with affection[1] the marks of his confidence, because this Chief Justice possessed the useful talent of bending and twisting the laws to every sort of iniquity.

The property of every government is to communicate to those who serve it its own reflex and colour; thus Charles lowered all men, and. blasted by his commissions the characters of those who, if better employed, would have become great citizens. For example, Churchill is sent by him to Louis XIV. to arrange the price of the dependency of the English crown; and the same Churchill, then the

[1] He loaded him with honours, and gave him a ring with his affection, when he set off to proceed with his most iniquitous judgments.

negociator of an ignoble treaty, was Marlborough, whose talents William III. and Queen Anne were able to turn to better account, for the glory of their country.

Charles, during twenty-five years, maintained a rule which had commenced amidst noisy acclamations of joy, and which ended in the silence of a sullen grief. Sad is the history of a reign which signalizes itself only by pslitieal law-suits, and dishonourable treaties, and which leaves behind it, to the people only the germ of a revolution, and to kings a disgraceful example.

"One is led to ask," says Boulay (de la Meurthe), " how so shameful a reign could last so long? It is only because the recollection of the years which preceded it was yet too general and too lively, and because the royalist party, elsewhere numerous, powerful, and well united, skilfully turned it to its own profit; it is because the friends of liberty, although much more numerous, were never agreed, either on the means to be employed, or on the end to be attained by their efforts; it is because the most odious transactions of Charles were unknown during his life; and it is because his falseness concealed the perfidy of his views; it is because cowardice

HISTORICAL FRAGMENTS.

~ him ,ir.lw ~ in rim~. ll&)ft th.an onee, before til~ ~.: mi wn..:di. ~ relliJ' to bani.··

Cb.ri~ II. J.:~ in 1,;;~). - Theee hue been, si:2.:cn J,la.~c.. - ~~ Ik~y li~ b lleurthe), - pr..:c.~ m,:re W:•~etl an.'l DI•M'I? ~71linary than !:..~: ~(U n,:c one, ——4·5-...-b.:- h."ti ~ t6 ;reater ~~-~ ~:c.:i:~_p, ~:.~ ~ Jme! and his d4.--nity." ~b~l~i.. i:.~ i&:..,;:..; iun E~~ an im~)nant and ~~ri·:~ r/;;.,; h~ bl ..Iy to 1~:,tit by Off'lllll- ~~ ;W:.J tt} ——-:c.,i t(· lh.~ n,:(\:~ unpalse ol the :..;iri:n. At t.·~- ~ fr¥.1~tl"'° t::,ur.d hiimeJ£. it ~ t~. in a ~=~i~:c. ~ itm~- l.b.u~ do what !:~ .-:..~J n ~ ,ci.~: j:,~r..m n.:g tu excite mudl L~.:-1:.te:.i: }..·u t.h~ £c~"1Y oi this position yas n a ~ n.~ i:i.5 t.\w"lt• ..:d. It mu..--t not be ~,r;:~~.n.. ~L ~=~ c,,y ~ immeese m~jority of the n.ui..:-n. and ..-itt..:-c.t tl.~ ai-.l ..:.f any to~on r-c,w-er!' be j:.a::.-d ~(on his return invested with I (')llll-l~ and a ~...._;.h m...,re than t'llO~,b to =:aim -.bar l'HIWDN (·t a...~ty. and. to ~Dffliate the minds (•f all. He ~~ f.:,r that purpoR a ::::: ==:::: :: ::: ::::, :haracter. and a little frankx: conduct.

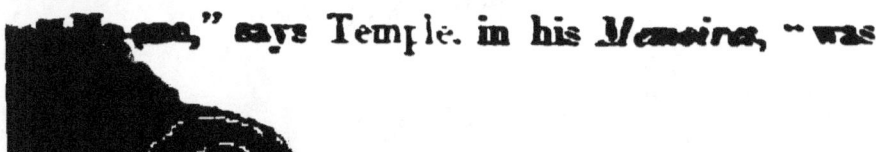

," says Temple. in his *Memoirs*, "was

more amiable, or of more easy access; far from being imposing or reserved, he had not the least leaven of pride or vanity. He was the most affable and civil of men. He treated his subjects less as vassals and tenants than as so many noblemen, gentlemen, or men of independence. His way of saying compliments was plausible, and all his manner engaging. He acquired an empire over the hearts, even whilst he was losing the esteem of his subjects, and frequently he made them hesitate between their judgment and their inclination."[1]

But M. de Chateaubriand depicts more philosophically than any other, in his *Melanges Historiquee,* the reign of Charles II. "This prince," says this great writer, " was one of those men who sometimes place themselves between two historic periods, to finish one and to commence the other, to deaden resentments, without being powerful enough to extinguish principles ; one of those princes whose reign serves as a passage or transition to great changes in the institutions, in the manners, and in the ideas of a people ; one of those princes created expressly to fill empty spaces, which, in the order of politics, often divide cause and effect."

[1] Hume, vol. x., p. 148.

CHAPTER V

CONCLUSION.

Let us sum up, in this last chapter, the causes of the fall of the Stuarts, and of the grandeur of William III.

The descendants of the unfortunate queen of Scotland had received from nature brilliant qualities ; they even possessed that affability of manner which wins men's hearts. William was dry, cold, reserved.

The reigns of the Stuarts always commenced under the most happy auspices ; everything appeared to smile on them. William, on the contrary, was from the first surrounded by dangers and difficulties without number. Why did the former fall with so many chances of success, whilst the latter triumphed with so many chances of being de troyed !

The Stuarts reached the throne at a period when the progress of civilization had divided England into two distinct parties : the ancient interests, strong by the consecration of time ; the new interests, strong by the ascendancy of reason.

Instead of uniting these two national interests, they supported only the ancient rights, and began the struggle. However, the general good could only result from the intimate fusion of these two causes; and, as all fusion requires fire to produce it, it was the civil war which charged itself with accelerating, under the Stuarts, a result which William obtained by his patriotism and genius.

The Stuarts found themselves always in a false position. Official representatives of Protestantism, they were Catholics at the bottom of their hearts. Compelled to be representatives of a system of liberty and of tolerance, they were absolute by instinct. Representatives of English interests, they were devoted or else sold to France.

William, on the contrary, was truly by nature and by conviction that which he represented on the throne.

By the manner in which the Prince of Orange established his authority, he was sure to have a marked advantage over the Stuarts. It was not Charles I. and James II., inheriting a power already despised and degraded; neither was *it* Charles II., called by the temporary accord of opposite parties, obliged to be either their plaything or their oppressor; it was the founder of a new order of things, the establishment of which had been hastened by his courage and skill.

The source whence any power is derived determines its duration, in the same way as an edifice stands through centuries or falls down in a few days, according as its foundation is well or ill laid.

In general, revolutions conducted and executed by a chief[1] turn entirely to the profit of the masses; for, to succeed, the chief is obliged to abound in the feeling of the nation entirely; and, to maintain himself, he must remain faithful to the interests which caused him to triumph; whilst, on the contrary, those revolutions which are made by the masses frequently profit only the chiefs, because the people believes on the morrow of its .victory that its

[1] It is clear that I only speak of those revolutions which occur in free countries, where moral force has greater power than physical.

work is accomplished, and that it is essential to repose for a long time after all the efforts that its victory required.

Thus, then, William III., who, not acquiring his power as heir, had nothing to bind him to the acts or principles of the preceding reigns ; who, in his own person and by his mighty deeds, was the head of his cause and of the revolution ; who, in fact, by his free election, had acquired an incontestable right, had laid deep in the English soil the basis of his throne.

Let us now consider the personal conduct of these different sovereigns.

The Stuarts had courage, spirit, perseverance; but they employed these qualities in opposing themselves to the wants of their people, and in opposition to circumstances.

They resisted where they should have yielded, and they yielded where resistance was a duty.

They were steadfast in their hatred, never in their affection; and when once drawn into the revolutionary vortex, they wanted that virtue which can alone save in great perils, magnanimity.

A tranquil and regular society may be governed by the gifts of the mind a.lone ; but when violence has taken the place of right, and the methodical progress of civilization has been broken, a sovereign cannot recover lost ground but by taking a great and sudden resolution, such as the heart alone inspires.

When Charles I., resisting the revolutionary torrent, was blockaded in Oxford, in 1644, by the parliamentary army, it was not by discussing minutely the prerogatives of the crown and the rights of the parliament, that he could regain his lost influence; but by taking one of those grand decisions which astonish by their audacity and please by their greatness, as, for example, presenting himself in London, alone, in person, trusting himself to the generosity of the people.'

When James II. learned the hostile projects of the Prince of Orange, it was not by imploring the

---

¹ The fears of our enemies sometimes show us, better than our own feelings, what are our real interests. In 1644, the Parliament believed that the King had the intention of coming to London to put himself at the head of the people of the city, who were devoted to him; it was seized with a panic fright, and took measures the most energetic to prevent Charles I. from realising a project which otherwise he never would have thought of (See Guizot, t. ii., p. 44).

assistance of Louis XIV. that he could strengthen his crown, but by ma.king an appeal to the fidelity of a free parliament, and by addressing to the country that lofty language which vibrates so well from the height of a throne.

Only when the powers are equally balanced can a strife be maintained for any length of time, and when, in the whirl of revolutions, vice and virtue, truth and error, are confused in their mutual onset, it is only by the generous passions of the soul that the hateful passions of parties can be quelled.

But the Stuarts had on the lips that which William had in the heart; they possessed that politeness of vice which imitates virtues which it has not, whilst William had that roughness of virtue which disdains all tinsel and all borrowed lustre.

Protestantism had become in England, since the sixteenth century, the emblem of all national interests. To be powerful internally as well as externally, the Stuarts had only to put themselves frankly at the head of this cause; far from that, they abandoned it abroad and used all their efforts to check it at home.

But there has never been, in the case of a free

people, a government sufficiently powerful long to repress liberty in the interior, without giving it glory abroad. Now the course of the government of the Stuarts manifested itself by daily contradictions which sometimes violated the rules of justice, sometimes the rules of politics.

Charles I., though entirely abandoning in Europe the Protestant cause, could not prevent the enlistment in his own dominions of partisans and soldiers for Gustavus Adolphus, that hero of Protastantism.

Charles II. was obliged, to satisfy public opinion, to give his niece to the Prince of Orange, head of the Protestant league ; James, although a Catholic and a persecutor, was constrained to give an asylum to the victims of the revocation of the edict of Nantes.

So that the Stuarts were ceaselessly awakening sympathies in favour of that cause which they wished to sacrifice, and their protection, far from being a sign of their generosity, was a proof of their weakness and cowardice.

But it is impossible to violate with impunity the people's logic. To maintain peace whilst arousing the symbols of war ; to protect the persecuted whilst making common cause with the persecutors ; charging the people with imposts, in order to make the fleets and the army be accessories to a shameful treaty; to stretch daily all the prerogatives of power, without even guaranteeing public tranquillity, these are inconsisUbcies for which the people, sooner or later, will call them to account.

Always in a state of hostility towards the nation, the Stuarts had recourse by turns to the laws and to men, to things the most holy or the most profane, as to arms of attack or of defence. Making use of Protestant ministers to re-establish Catholicism, and sending Catholics to the scaffold; making use of political men to overthrow the Parliament, and then abandoning them immediately to parliamentary vengeance, they were constantly impeded in their projects, constantly drawn into paths quite contrary to their desires, and appeared to have no object because they dared not avow the true one.

The Stuarts never sought by the application of what grand principle, by the adoption of what great system they might ensure the prosperity and the preponderance of their country ; but by what crafty expedients, by what hidden intrigues, they might sustain their ever-embarrassed power. They never sought *by u:kat means,* but *by whom* they should be able to maintain themselves, always thus putting private interest in the place of general interest, personal questions in the room of questions of principles, and intrigue in the place of lofty political conceptions.

William, on the contrary, put under foot all obstacles, and made all diverse opinions, as also all opposed individuals concur, for one single purpose, the interest of the country.

The Stuarts only made war for the purpose of sustaining by a little glory their tottering power.

William made war to increase the influence of England.

After their defeats, the Stuarts demanded peace; William accepted it, only after a victory.

The greatest reproach that can be brought against the two last Stuarts, is that they were always the slaves of Louis XIV. When they found themselves in a difficulty, they called for the assistance of a foreigner, forgetting that often men pardon everything in a sovereign, excepting hie not being true to his country.

All men, great and little, place their honour

somewhere. The Stuarts placed their honour as a relic in the holy ark of royal prerogatives. William placed his in national pride.

Here below, all men are more or less actors ; but each one chooses his theatre and his auditory, and directs all his efforts, all well as all his ambition, towards the attainment of the suffrages of this pit of his own selection; like to Alexander, who, on the banks of the Indus, was wont to think the approbation of the Athenians would be the most delightful recompense of his labours.

The Stuarts only ambitioned the praise of a faction and of a foreign sovereign. William, on the contrary, made his glory. consist in meriting the approbation of posterity.

Whilst the first knew not how to profit by the goods of the earth under a cloudless sky, the second knew how to gather in a harvest whilst a tempest was raging.

The Stuarts assembled the Parliament to deceive it, William to convince it. The first dissolved or prorogued the Houses each time that they spoke of national honour or liberty ; the second dlssolved them when they were animated by reactionary passions or by sentiments opposed to the glory of the country.

The Stuarts reigned by dissimulation and intrigue ; William governed by frankness. The Stuarts always made a great noise when they gave their alarms, in order to conceal their culpable hopes. William a.vowed boldly his hopes to dissipate alarms.

Whilst the Stuarts were hesitating, William was marching.

Whilst the Stuarts, ruled by the crowd, saw nothing around them but confusion, William had already perceived the end to which matters tended, rushed forward and drew the crowd after him.

The example of these unfortunate kings proves that when a governmen~ combats the ideas and the wishes of a nation, it always produces a result the very opposite of what it had calculated.

The Stuarts desired to re-establish Catholicism ; they destroyed it for centuries to come in England. They wished to raise again royalty ; they compromised it. They desired to ensure order, and they brought about convulsion after convulsion. It is then true to say that : " The greatest enemy of a religion is he who is determined to impose it ; the greatest enemy to royalty, he who degrades it; the greatest enemy to the repose of his country, he who renders a revolution necessary."

William III. succeeded in closing the gulf of revolutions and securing the destinies of England; only because his conduct was quite the opposite to that of the Stuarts; for if he had followed the same errors, and walked in the same traces, he would have compromised the safety of all that he, as it was, consolidated.

Let us consider, indeed, what would have resulted if the Prince of Orange, after having dethroned James II. and violated the hereditary principle, had accepted the crown from the last parliament of James II., and if instead of convoking a. national convention, a free expression of the popular will, he had only held his authority from an illegal assembly who had not any right to give it him.

Let us suppose that instead of destroying the treaties of the Stuarts, he had implored like them the support and the goodwill of a foreign power;

Let us suppose that instead of sustaining, arms in his hand, the Protestant cause on the continent, he had abandoned it ;

Let us suppose that, without avenging England of all the affronts which it had received, he had kept in London a standing army more numerous than the troops of James II., only to intimidate the Parliament and to suffer humiliations abroad ; that instead of folJowinga great aim, he had only made, like the Stuarts, useless expeditions, for the purpose of deceiving military ardour and of making a diversion in public opinion ;

Let us suppose that instead of taking as his basis the general interests, he had equally wounded the ancient interests and the modem interests ; that he had, like the Stuarts, broken his oath to the men who had aided him, and had been faithless to the promises which he had sanctioned in his manifesto; that instead of uttering in the Houses of Parliament a language full of dignity, he had only appealed to vulgar sentiments, to base passions, and to fears of anarchy, pointing to these fears as a justification of the tyrannical acts of the preceding reigns; [1]

Let us suppose, finally, that instead of strengthening the cause of the revolution of 1688, he had betrayed it ; that instead of raising the name of

---

[1] If, for example, the Parliament had accepted the responsibility of the judicial murder of Lord Russell and Sidney, instead of doing justice to its memory, as it did.

England, he had abased it ; that instead of lightening the condition of the people, he had burdened it with imposts, without increasing either its glory, or its commerce, or its industry ; that he had restrained its libert.ies, without even guaranteeing public order; it is certain that a new revolution would have become an imperious necessity. For societies do not undergo those overthrows which often compromise their existence, merely to change a chief; they arouse themselves to change a system, to heal their sufferings ; they imperiously demand the reward of their efforts, and do not calm themselves until they have obtained it.

William III. satisfied the requirements of his period and re-established public tranquillity ; but if he had followed the policy of the Stuarts, he would have been overthrown, and the enemies of the English nation, again seeing that new changes were called for, would have accused the people of inconsistency and frivolity, instead of charging its governors with blindness and perfidy ; they would have said that England was an ungovernable nation; they would have termed it, as James II. named it in his " Memoirs," *an eneenomed nation.* But, in spite of these accusations, the national cause, sooner or later, would have triumphed, for God and reason would have been on its side!

Let us say, in conclusion, that from a study of these periods which we have recalled, we derive principles clear, precise, and applicable to all countries.

The example of the Stuarts proves that *fore'ign aid is always incompetent to ease tkose go,oernments wkick tke nation will not adopt.*

And the History of England speaks loudly to kings:-

WALK AT THE HEAD OF THE IDEAS OF YOUR AGE, THOSE IDEAS WILL FOLLOW AND WILL SUSTAIN YOU.

WALK BEHIND THRM, THEY WILL DRAG YOU ALONG.

WALK IN OPPOSITION TO THEM, THEY WILL OVERTHROW YOU.

OUR COLONIES IN THE PACIFIC OCEAN.

* * * *

Unfortunately, in the actual state of Europe, France cannot extend, without inconvenience, her rule over isolated territories. Instead of scattering her forces, she must concentrate them : instead of wasting her treasure, she must economize it, for the day may come when she will require all her children and all her resources ; and the distant possessions, burdensome in time of peace, causes of disasters in time of war, are productive of weakness instead of being a germ of prosperity.

Two motives have always presided ever the establishment of colonies; to further the interest of war or that of commerce.

• * • *

If we were to be engaged in war, we should require for the defence of our colonies the following troops: for Algiers, sixty thousand men: for Guadeloupe and Martinique, ten thousand men: for Guiana, five thousand men: for Bourbon, three thousand men; for the African Station, two thousand men; for the Marquesas and Society Islands, ten thousand. As to Pondichery and Chandernagor, it would not be easy to estimate how many would be required to resist the imposing forces of the English in India. This would make a total of about a hundred thousand men, without reckoning the vessels, the *ma'tiriel,* and, consequently, the money which these armaments would cost.

* * • *

The more France extends her colonies, instead of developing those which she already possesses, the more she weakens her power.

In short, there are only two colonies of much importance: Algeria and Guiana.

* * * *

(Progr~, du Pas-de-Oalais, 14th June, 1841.)

UNION GIVES STRENGTH.

A LESSON DERIVED FROM HISTORY.

In 1685, the throne of England was held by a king who was called James II. This prince was simple in his manners, free from vices, and gifted with private qualities worthy of commendation.

When he came to the throne, people recalled with interest all the vicissitudes of his past life. They remembered that, whilst still young, he had fought with courage during the times of civil disturbance, and that, exiled with his family during the Republic and Protectorate, he had been brought up in the school of misfortune, which is always spoken of highly, but which is so often productive of no good results. Having reached the age when experience and reason ought to take the place of deceptive illusions and fiery passions, he gave himself out as the man most able to secure the welfare of the people he was called upon to govern.

However, it turned out quite otherwise. James TI. was the most hateful king England has ever had ; for there was nothing English about him, neither spirit, nor heart, nor interests, nor religion; even his qualifications were the reverse of suitable to the nation.

England was a municipal country, he was an advocate of centralization; she was constitutional, he was a despot; she was Protestant, he was Catholic; she was proud and independent, he was humble and the slave of a foreigner.

The great political events which, when Duke of York, the king had witnessed, instead of creating in him profound convictions based upon the terrible examples of his predecessors, had left no traces in him except hatred of the new ideas and doubt even as to what is· good. He called progress an utopian conception; glory, a chimera; honour, a prejudice ; the misery of the poorer classes, an unfortunate necessity. Persuaded that, in the eyes of God, the prerogatives of the crown were of higher value than the rights of the people; that. the liberties and the cause for which the English nation had been fighting for forty years were dear only to a small number of factious men who were corrupting the public mind ; that the institutions, which sprang from the revolution, were perpetually menacing his authority,[1] he resolved to restore by craft. or by force, in all their integrity, the old abuses, the old customs, and the ancient dogma.

To succeed in this treacherous project he reckoned upon the moral prostration of the nation, on the help of a foreign power, on the division of political parties, on the army, and on the resources of his spirit of dissimulation.

At this period there was a general apathy throughout the nation ; the political changes which had occurred during the short space of fifty years had destroyed weight of character, weakened beliefs, and almost destroyed public opinion. Parties, though they had become less violent, kept up the same feeling of animosity towards each other, and, by their division, handed over the country to a sect without honour and without patriotism. " There was," says Hallam (*Constitutional Hinor9,* vol. iii.,

---

[1] James II. would often say, that no government could exjt with institutions such as the Habeas Corpus and the Test Act.-(Dalrymple, p. 171.)

p. 75), "a great relaxation of principles in the upper classes, and, in the lower classes, a servile dependance on power and an immoderate thirst for places," So much so that James II. said to Berillon, the ambassador, his confidant (Hallam, p. 76), "that he had sufficient experience of England to know that the chance of having employments and offices would make more Catholics than would the permission to perform mass in public,"

Parliament was the faithful reflex of the nation's state of atrophy. There was neither a complete adhesion to the measures of government, nor a compact and national opposition, consequently, no decisive majority. A law of the most important nature passed by the majority of one only (Hallam, p. 82). So the people contemplated the debates in the Houses, 38 they look on at a cock-fight, bestowing unbounded preises on the conqueror whoever he might be.

In the meantime, the policy of James II. every day increased the number of his enemies. In home affairs there was nothing but arbitrary conduct and corruption ; abroad, nothing but weakness and cowardice. The first act of the king, as he mounted the throne, had been to beg for a subsidy from a foreign sovereign. Afterwards, insurrections having broken out in some parts of the kingdom, he made them a pretext for keeping on foot the most numerous army England ever had.

Although the king's government was at peace with all powers, Great Britain resounded with warlike beatings of drums and flourishes of trumpets ; but this army, which, under the Republic and the Protectorate, had caused the English name to be respected over the whole of the continent, had now no higher mission than the maintaining of a policy the most disgraceful with which the country had ever been afflicted. Moreover, the officers were chosen, not because of warlike qualifications, but according to their political views. (Hallam, p. 75.)

We have an example of the way in whieh power was employed, in the following extract from one of Barillon's letters: "It seemed to me," said the ambassador, "that the king was very glad to have a pretext for raising troops. He believes that the enterprize of the Duke of Monmouth will only help to make him still more master of his country. His project is to disband the militia regiments entirely, the danger and uselessness of which he has recognized on this late occasion. He very well knows that the Parliament will not view with pleasure this establishment, but he wishes to make sure of the interior of his country and believes he can do so in no other way." (Dalrymple, p. 169.)

In fact, a man must reign either by moral force or by brutal. James II. chose the latter line. and he believed that with a yielding Parliament, with a body of devoted judges, at the head of whom were Herbert and Jefferies, with a standing army, he could be master of the bodies and souls of his subjects, that is to say, of laws and of men's consciences. He had a bill passed for the preservation of the king's person, which, says Hallam (p. 71), was full of dangerous innovations and of unconstitutional "enactments. He violated the freedoms of corporations *(l!'orfeitures of Corporations,* Hallam, P: 70). He limited the rights of election; and even the Uni varsity of Oxford, that sanctuary of royalist ideas, was not protected from his arbitrary proceedings. Public opinion was loudly raised against the dismissal of the professors of Magdalene College. People openly said on this occasion (Hallam, P: 104): "What have we gained by our revolutions, if Ja~es IL thinks he can govern as despotically as the Tudors *i"*

The composition of the Privy Council, the members of which were selected from amongst the most unpopular men, irritated the whole nation " which learnt," says Hallam (p. 79), "with indignation and even with contempt that a minister without principles, an intriguing bishop, or a licentious poet had passed over to the side of a monarch whose favor could not be obtained unless at the sacrifice of a man's political and religious belief." Nevertheless, on the appearance of the famous decree of liberty of conscience which so strongly aroused public opinion, the constituted bodies were so degraded by the habit of submission that congratulatory addresses were sent in hundreds by all the sects, by all the grand juries, corporations, towns and villages. These addresses, always deceptive homage when coming from an oppressed people, were renewed with the same apparent fervour on the occasion of the birth of the Prince of Wales, and "now that we know the prevailing spirit of the people at that time," says the English historian (Hallam, p. 101), "we should be forced to blush on account of the cowardice and hypocrisy of our ancestors, if we did not understand that these addresses were after all the work of a very small number of men."

The foreign policy of James II. was as severely criticised as his management of the home affairs of the nation. At this time the League of Augsbourg had been formed to resist the ambition of Louie XIV. England, a free country, a Protestant and maritime power, was by nature the rival of France, and deeply interested in the independence of the Low Countries. She should have placed herself at the head of this league ; u But the sinister inelinations of the king," says Hallam, " had separated him from the real interests of his people, and had made him the vassal of a foreign sovereign." His ministers used to boast of the Anglo-French alliance, and Sunderland at this time wrote to the ambassador of France (Hallam, p. 75): "I see clearly the apprehension which many people entertain with respect to an intimate alliance with France, and the efforts that are made to weaken it ; but it will be out of any one's power to do that." These words show us in what a state of blindness the English court was living; and by what means could it have aroided the catastrophe which awaited it, when it had no loyalty in its diplomatic intercourse, even with the power to which it was most. indebted / Whilst James II. was plotting with Barillon against the liberties of his people, and was addressing to Louis XIV. protestation after protestation, he was secretly treating for an alliance with Spain (Hallam, p. 108).

There is one very remarkable fact to be recorded under this reign, one which proves how powerless governments are when they choose to oppose the general sentiment of a country. It is quite possible for them temporarily to repress insurrections, to stifle complaints, to corrupt individuals; but what they gain on the one hand they are obliged to restore on the other; whatever they, by force, will not allow to live in deeds, will only bud and develop itself in the domain of thought.

It is eurions to see that this English monarch, the vassal of Louis XIV., wishing to destroy in his own country the Protestant religion and liberty, has not power enough, notwithstanding his troops, his judges, his courtiers, to refuse an asylum to the victims of the edict of Nantes, who brought into his own land a spirit of reform and of liberty which he was so anxious to destroy.

However, notwithstanding the ever-increasing unpopularity of the King's government, the spirit of the nation had degenerated to such an extent, that it is allowable to believe his projects would have succeeded if a happy transformation had not taken place in the parties which then divided England. So long as the Anglicans, the Nonconformists, the Dissenters, the Whigs, and the Tories, waged a fratricidal war, the ruling power gained strength by their division; and public opinion, unguided, floated as uncertainly as a ship without compass and without a helmsman. What, in fact, can be more deplorable than to aee parties tearing each other to pieces in a strife of words about mystical theories, whilst they are at the bottom of it all agreed as to the grand fundamental principles which, if generally adopted, would secure the future well-being of the country? There was one point on which all parties should have come to an understanding ; for all, with the exception of the one who ruled, wished for the liberty and the glory of England ; and again, all recognized the will of the people as the supreme judge ; and freedom of election, as the means by which a good understanding could be effected between the children of one and the same great family.

Unhappily, parties, like individuals, may be bound together by a common antipathy more easily than by a reciprocal sympathy; and, although they all had in the depth of their hearts the same love, it was hatred of an anti-national power which ranged them under the same standard. From that time the cause of James II. was irretrievably lost, and that of the English people irrevocably won. In vain the king boasted that he was surrounded by men who had served, each in its turn, the Republic, Cromwell, and Charles II. ; these men represented no party, no interest--for deserters never carry with them their standards. There were no longer more than two parties in England ; the one, composed of the men on the side of power, men without principle, without conscience, without national sympathies ; the other, composed of all that the country contained of men sworn to secure the reign of liberty, of independence, and the greatness of their fatherland. Protestantism was then, in England, the symbol of all these great interests, and, in order to insure their triumph, Puritans and Anglicans, republicans and royalists, they all united against the common enemy. From this union sprang, radiant and full of promise, the celebrated revolution of 1688. It required many tears, much bloodshed, and, above all, many years, to obtain this immense result, *for, ,ince Ike R68toration, twent,9-eigkt 9ear, kad paued away* !

IMPROVEMENTS

TO BB INTRODUCSD INTO

OUR PARLIAMENTARY MANNERS AND HABITS.

*   *   *   *

In England, the majority of important questions, before being carried into Parliament, have been fathomed and discussed in many public or private meetings, which are like so many machines, sifting, breaking, pounding political materials, before they pass through the great parliamentary rolling-mill.

*   *   *   *

It is worth noticing that the habit which our neighbours have of depriving themselves of the society of ladies in their clubs and after dinner, is not without its influence on the development of public opinion, for it is the absence of ladies which permits the men daily to discuss serious questions.

*   *   *   *

(Progr~s du Pas-de-Calais, 18th Sept., 1843.)

PEACE.

People are incessantly repeating to us that peace is a blessing and war a scourge. But one thing is not said often enough, which is, if war is often a necessity when a great cause has to be defended, it is, on the other hand, a great crime to make it from caprice, without having a grand result in view, an immense advantage to justify it.

• • • •

In our eyes, peace is the harmony resulting from difficulties smoothed down, opposing interests satisfied; it is the most complete security reigning in society. Nothing of this kind exists at the present time.

• • •

To insure peace, we must have an equitable and elevated policy, we must dare to avow it openly and defend it with vigour ; we must give to foreign nations a great idea of the good faith and of the strength of France, showing by our actions that we have no desire of making conquests.

But the government, for forty years, has been pursuing an entirely contrary course. Instead of showing itself inflexible and not to be moved in maintaining its rights, it has always abandoned them whenever they have been called in question ; instead of earning the confidence of Europe by its conduct, it has incessantly disquieted it by undertaking some conquests or some expeditions which disturbed the general harmony without increasing the influence of our country.

By this mistaken policy, the French cabinet has drawn upon itself, justly, the distrust of France as well as that of foreign powers ; it has awakened jealousies and hatreds which were asleep.

Abroad, men question the good faith of a government which, notwithstanding its promises, cannonaded Lisbon, took Ancona, bombarded the ports of .Mexico, excited the Pacha of Egypt to revolt., fomented the disturbances in Spain, took possession of the islands of the Marquesas and of Talti, and needlessly bombarded Tangier and Mogador.

Foreign statesmen cried out, "Look at these

Frenchmen ! They are always tormented by the same ambition ; the only way of governing them is to fascinate their eyes with military glory. Have we not a proof of it, when we see their present rulers, eminently men of peace, are themselves obliged, in order to sustain themselves, to seek on all continents and on all seas some small military or naval successes!"

• • • •

To insure peace, is not to maintain during a few years a fictitious tranquillity; it is to labour to dissipate hatreds between nations, by favouring the interests, the natural tendency of each people-it is to create a just balance of the great powers; it is, in a word, to follow the policy of Henry IV. and not the disastrous course of the Stuarts and of Louis XV.

* * * *

To establish a European balance firmly, Henry IV. foresaw that it was necessary that all nations should be equal in power, and that no one of them should preponderate over the rest ; he foresaw that, for peoples as well as for individuals, equality is the only source of justice. Henry IV. had brought the greater part of Europe to second him in his humane views; and, when the steel of a cowardly assassin cut short his days so valuable, he was assembling an immense army composed of European contingents, proposing as his aim, not a sterile ,conquest, but universal peace. He was about to force Spain to recognize the equality and independence of nations, and he would have established a sort of areopagus designed to put an end, by reason and not by brutal force, to the quarrels between people and people. Henry IV., had he lived, might have been surnamed, with truth, the hero of peace.

With this grand project let ns compare the wretched policy of the two last Stuarts. These, plunging England, wearied with revolutions, into an ignoble torpor, gave up to the foreigner the interests and the honour of their country ; they reigned by means of peace, but their conduct, so antinational, brought about, as was sure to be the case, a re-action which gave birth to a war of twenty-five years.

*   *   *   *

For a few years there existed no more rivalry between France and England ; both these nations seemed about to march side by side in the path of prf>gress; to-day the gonrnment has so managed that, on the one hand by its attac~ and on the other by iis eoneessions, it has again aroused all the sentimenta of jealousy between the two nations; it ha... recalled to life ancient esuses of complaint., and if eTer the fire bursts out, our gonrnment it is whieh will be the eanse of it, for it, and no other, will have collected the combustible materials.

● ● ● ●

The veritable author of war, a celebrated writer ii,ays, is not the man who declares it, bnt the man who has made it necessary by a policy without sr-eatness, without dignity, without good faith.

Progr~, du Paa-de-Calail, Nov. 5, 1844.

END OF EXTRACTS.

LIMITS OF FRANCE

AS DEFINED BY

THE TREATY OF PARIS.

SIGNED MAY 80, 1814,

CONFIRMED BY CONGRESS OF VIENNA,

JUNE 9, 1815.

LIMITS OF FRANCE.

At the present moment it may be interesting to the public to have an extract from the Treaty of Paris, of May 30, 1814, showing in what way the boundaries of that kingdom were settled ; and afterwards confirmed by the Vienna Congress, June 9, 1815. The parties to the Treaty of Vienna, were, Austria, Spain, France, England, Portugal, Prussia, Russia, Sweden, and Norway.

ARTICLE II. *(of tke Paris Treaty.)*

The kingdom of France retains its limits entire, as they existed on Jan\lary 1, 1792. It shall further receive the increase of territory comprised within the line established by the following Article:-

ARTICLE Ill.

On the side of Belgium, Germany, and Italy, the ancient frontiers shall be re-established as they existed J a.nuary 1, 1 792, extending from the

North Sea, between Dunkirk and Nieuport, to the Mediterranean between Cagnes and Nice, with the following modifications:-

1. In the department of Jemappes, the Cantons of Dour, Merbes-le-Chateau, Beaumont, and Chimay, shall belong to France ; where the line of demarcation comes in contact with the Canton of Dour, it shall pass between that Canton and those of Boussu and Paturage, and likewise further on it shall pass between the Canton of Merbes-le-Chateau and those of Bink and Thuin.

2. In the department of Sambre and Meuse, the Cantons of Walcourt, Florennes, Beauraing, and Gedinne, shall belong to France ; where the demarcation reaches that department, it shall follow the line which separates the said Cantons from the department of Jemappes, and from the remaining Cantons of the department of Sambre and Mense.

3. In the department of the Moselle, the new demarcation, at the point where it diverges from the old line of frontier, shall be formed by a line to be drawn from Perle to Fremersdorff, and by the limit which separates the Canton of Tholey from the remaining Cantons of the said department of the Moselle.

4. In the department of La Sarre, the Cantons of Saarbruck and Arneval shall continue to belong to France, as likewise the portion of the Canton of Lebach which is situated to the south of a line drawn along the confines of the villages of Herchenbaeh, Ueberhofen, Hilsbach, and Hall (leaving these different places out of the French frontier), to the point where, in the neighbourhood of Querselle (which place belongs to France) the line which separates the Cantons of Arneval and Ottweiler reaches that which separates the Cantons of Arneval and Lebach. The frontier on this side shall be formed by the line above described, and afterwards by that which separates the Canton of Arneval from that of Bliescastel.

5. The fortress of Landau having, before the year 1792, formed an insulated point in Germany, France retains beyond her frontiers a portion of the departments of Mount Tonnerre and of the Lower Rhine, for the purpose of uniting the said fortress and its radius to the rest of the kingdom.

The new demarkation from the point in the neighbourhood of Obersteinbach (which place is left out of the limits of France) where the boundary between the department of the Moselle and that of

Mount Tonnerre reaches the department of the Lower Rhine, shall follow the line which separates the cantons of Weissenbourg and Bergzabern (on the side of France) from the Cantons of Permasens Dahn, and Annweiler (on the side of Germany) as far as the point near the village of Vollmersheim, where that line touches the ancient radius of the fortress of Landau. From this radius, which remains as it was in 1792, the new frontier shall follow the arm of the river de la. Queich, which, on leaving the said radius at Queichheim (that place remaining to France), flows near the villages of Merlenheim, Knittelsheim, and Belheim (these places also belong to France) to the Rhine, which from thence shall continue to form the boundary of France and Germany.

The main stream (Thalweg) of the Rhine shall constitute the frontier, provided, however, that the changes which may hereafter take place in the course of that river shall not affect the property of the islands. The right of possession in these islands shall be re-established as it existed at the signature of the treaty of Luneville.

6. In the department of the Doubs, the frontier shall· be so regulated as to commence above the

Baneonnlere, near Locle, and follow the crest of Jura between the Cemeux, Pequignot, and the village of Fontanelles, as far as the peak of that mountain, situated about seven or eight thousand feet to the north-west of the village of La Brevine, where it shall again fall in with the ancient boundary of France.

7. In the department of the Leman, the frontiers between the French territory, the Pays de Vaud and the different portions of the territory of the republic of Geneva (which is to form part of Swisserland) remain as they were before the incorporation of Geneva with France. But the Cantons of Frangy and of St. Julien (with the exception of the districts situated to the north of a line drawn from the point where the river of *La Loire* enters the territory of Geneva, near Chancy, following the confines of Sesequin, Laconex, and Seseneuve, (which shall remain out of the limits of France) the Canton of Reignier, with the exception of the portion to the east of a line which follows the confines of the Muraz Bussy, Pers, and Cornier (which shall be out of the French limits) and the Canton of La Roche (with the exception of the places called La Roche, and Armanoy, with their districts) shall

remain to France. The frontier shall follow the limits of these different Cantons, and the line which separates the districts continuing to belong to France, from those which she does not retain.

In the department of Mont Blanc, France acquires the sub-prefecture of Chambery, with the exception of the Cantons of L'Hepital, St. Pierre d'Albigny, la. Rocette, and Montmelian, and the sub-prefecture of Annecy, with the exception of the portion of the Canton of Faverges, situated to the east of a line passing between Ourecha.ise and Marlens on the side of France, and Ma.rthod and Ugine on the opposite side, and which afterwards follows the crest of the mountains as far as the frontier of the Canton of Thones ; this line, together with the limit of the Cantons before mentioned, shall on this side form the new frontier.

On the side of the Pyrenees, the frontiers between the two kingdoms of France and Spain, remain such as they were on January 1, 1792, and a joint commission shall be named on the pa.rt of the two crowns, for the purpose of finally determining the line.

France on her pa.rt renounces all rights of Sovereignty, *luzerainetl,* and of possession over all the countries, districts, towns, and places, situated beyond the frontier above described, the Principality of Monaco being replaced on the same footing on which it stood before January 1, 1792.

The Allied Powers assure to France the possession of the Principality of Avignon, of the Comtat Venaissin, of the Comte of Montbeilliard, together with the several insulated territories which formerly belonged to Germany, comprehended within the frontier above described, whether they have been incorporated with France before or after January 1, 1792. The Powers reserve to themselves, reciprocally, the complete right to fortify any point in their respective states which they may judge necessary for their security.

To prevent all injury to private property, and protect, according to the most liberal principles, the property of individuals domiciliated on the frontiers, there shall be named, by each of the states bordering on France, commissioners, who shall proceed, conjointly with French commissioners, to the delineation of the respective boundaries.

As soon as the commissioners shall have performed their task, maps shall be drawn, signed by the respective commissioners, and posts shall be placed to point out the reciprocal boundaries.

ARTICLE IV.

To secure the communications of the town of Geneva. with other parts of the Swiss territory situated on the lake, France consents that the road by Versoy shall be common to the two countries. The respective governments shall amicably arrange the means for preventing smuggling, regulating the posts, and maintaining the said road.

THE GENERAL TREATY OF VIENNA.

The Powers who signed the Treaty concluded at Paris in May 80, 1814, having assembled at Vienna, in pursuance of Article 82 of that Act, embraced in one· common transaction, the various results of their negociatfons, for the purpose of confirming them by their reciprocal ratifications, and authorised their plenipotentiaries to unite, in a genera.I instrument, the regulations of superior and permanent interest, and to join to that act, as integral parts of the arrangements of Congress, the treaties, conventions, declarations, regulations, &c., as cited in this General Treaty : signed June 9, 1815.

www.ingramcontent.com/pod-product-compliance
Lightning Source LLC
Chambersburg PA
CBHW020830230426
43666CB00007B/1170